"A rare combination of brilliance and love combined with skills that have taken years to master."

–Doug Allen, Entrepreneur

"Tiffany Silver gets right to the point and facilitates direct personal / spiritual / psychological insight. She demonstrates with tools that enable anyone who truly wants clearer and better outcomes in their life exactly how to create them – immediately."

–Bill Quateman, CEO, Personalized Nutrition Consultants

"Tiffany passionately and powerfully assists others along their path of growth, healing and self-awareness. She skillfully uses her training, intuitive abilities and love to facilitate change in the world, one person at a time. I am so happy to know that people like Tiffany are on the planet!

–Virja Ma, Healer & Somatic Spiritual Life Coach

SILVER TO GOLD

THE ALCHEMY OF THE
FEMININE HEART.

Tiffany Silver

Silver to Gold – The Alchemy of the Feminine Heart

SILVER TO GOLD
THE ALCHEMY OF THE FEMININE HEART.

Books may be purchased by contacting the publisher at:
TiffanySilverLove.com/publications

Cover Design and Illustrations: Leanne Savage (worldstudios.carbonmade.com)

Cover Photo by Javiera Estrada (javieraphotography.com)

Edited by Gaynor Foster (consciousmedia.com.au)

Publisher: TiffanySilverLove (Santa Monica, CA)
ISBN: 978-0-9914309-0-1
10 9 8 7 6 5 4 3 2 1

1. Body, Mind, Spirit 2. Inspirational & Personal Growth

First Edition

Printed in the USA by TiffanySilverLove

Table of Contents

DEDICATION 7

INTRODUCTION TO TIFFANY SILVER 11

CHAPTER 1   THE KEYS TO LOVING OPENLY 17

CHAPTER 2:   NO MISTAKES: HUMANITY VS. DIVINITY 45

CHAPTER 3:   PERCEPTIONS ARE EVERYTHING.... 65

CHAPTER 4:   PRACTICAL TOOLS FOR THE LIFE YOU CRAVE......82

CHAPTER 5:   VICTIMHOOD / BLAME GAME / RESISTANCE..........109

CHAPTER 6:   RELATIONSHIPS 141

CHAPTER 7:   SELF-DISCOVERY 189

CHAPTER 8:   BEING YOUR OWN ORACLE..202

CHAPTER 9:   PROSPERITY 206

CHAPTER 10: CHANGE IS THE ONLY CONSTANT.............................210

CHAPTER 11: EMPOWER YOUR LIFE 237

CHAPTER 12: DREAMS 245

CHAPTER 13: C.H.O.I.C.E. 255

CHAPTER 14: EXPERIENCE LIFE 265

DEDICATION

I dedicate this book to my father and mother first and foremost, for being my greatest inspirations. Our interactions paved the way, and the benefits were innumerable. I love you Mom & Dad, just as you are.

Jeff my sweet friend, you continue to inspire me throughout the years, thru and thru I feel this book is the result of our endless hours of deep introspection into the human heart and mind and how it really aligns. I love your dedication to uplifting humanity by knowing your own divinity and always bringing the focus back to "god is supply". You have been my best friend, and I am the better version of myself due to your unconditional love and support. Forever in my heart and grateful for the time shared in discovering what it means to love freely.

I have to thank my editor, Gaynor Foster. This book would not be in your hands today if it wasn't for her attention, skill, dedication and belief in this project. Gaynor, you changed my life by allowing me to share this book in the world in such a seamless fashion, taking my writing to a new level and sharing our united voice as a team. I am forever grateful to you for your time and energy.

I could dedicate a whole new book to each one of these people so I am placing you in one paragraph together to emphasize how very important you are in my life. Lavinia and Christy, you two amazing soul sisters have supported me beyond measure and my love for you both is infinite. Laurin, Michelle and Doug, you all raised my standards and showed me a new level of myself that was awaiting your arrival in my life. Kelly, Tom, Elissa, and Keith: Your friendship showed me a new level of unconditional love. What I treasure most is that you all gave me your time, energy, heart, and your presence. This is priceless and precious to me. Our sharing brought some of the most pleasurable moments in my life. You have all touched my soul in countless ways and will remain forever in my heart together or apart, you are a piece of me. Thank you from the depths of my heart and soul for our profound, loving and meaningful exchanges. I am forever changed because each one of you opened my heart to be the best version of me and to reflect that back into each one of you. I love you all so much, my spiritual soul family!

Thank you Neal for your unconditional love and support always. You have given to me in ways that are priceless. Your friendship, love, care, and generosity have allowed me to follow my heart and share my love with the world. You demonstrate what it means to give unconditionally; this has touched me on so many levels. Our exchange has truly been a godsend!

I have to give Leanne, my graphic designer, my utmost appreciation. She conveyed exactly what I wanted to share through her artistic vision and beautiful open warm heart. Javiera, a master at her trade in photography, always captures a person's true essence. She has been an amazing longtime friend who opened my heart and continues to weave her magic in my life in all that I do. Thank you my dear Javiera with all my heart for your patience, friendship and unconditional love.

Thanks to marketing strategist, Gentry Smith of ibc-productions.com, for his creative collaboration, book interior layout and design work.

I must thank Dr. Sai-Ling Michael for the continued support in keeping me focused, in alignment, in love and always accelerating toward actualizing my potential. You have been the backbone to my success literally, and I am forever grateful for the years shared as I've grown and learned so much from you. Thank you to Dr.

Drew Hall very much for your care and for keeping my head on straight. I also want to thank Ed Japange of lifebeatproductions.com for his amazing healing tools that create neurological coherency. I've used these tools exclusively for over five years and they have aided me in being clear, grounded and effective.

Thank you, Dr. Sarah Larsen for being an angel and guiding me on the path to my many adventures around the world. It has been an honor receiving your love. You are forever in my heart with gratitude.

I have to thank Dr. Antonia Ruhl for being a guiding light and connector on my path. Her love fills my heart with joy. She is one of my emissaries of light, having brought pivotal people to bring this project to completion. Thank you my dear sister.

There are so many people who have contributed to bringing this book to fruition – the names are countless, as I believe everyone I've ever crossed paths with over the sum total of my life had an influence on who I've become and who I continue to become. So here's my dedication to the beloveds in my life who believed in me, for those who saw me and empowered my gifts, and strengthened my learning opportunities along the way:

My mother; my father; My Siblings: David, Jason, Danielle, Hannah; Jeff K; Christy E; Doug A; Sarah L; Laurin S; Tom M; Gaynor F; Michelle E; Kelly F-C; Javiera E; Sai-Ling M; Ed J; Elissa S; Drew H; Tony S; Wayne F; Carlos; Hindy Z; Nicole P; Jillian S; Keith L; Philippo F; Ryan P; Rainbeau M; Walker W; Karen S; Peter S; Lawrence B; Susanna H; Wonder B; Jacqueline V; John C; Tara S; Dick S; Donald S; Evan P; Angelica P; Alejandro F; Antonio R; Jose; Ana S; Andreia M; Brooke B; Antonia D-R; Tiffany R; Leanne S; Krista A; Jim C; Jason B; Hemalaya B; Anandagiri-ji; Ashwin; Kamala D; Judy S; Jasmine

S; Malaena M; Viraja P; Dave C; Melanie C; Rob L; Larry R; Ryan; Gabriella C; Gabriella T; Lawrence B; Tina P; Lauren S; Joaquin A; Paulette O; Harry P; Gentry S; Andrea D; Hilary G; The Hamrell family; every healer who guided me on my path; the Oneness community; all my amazing yoga guides (you know who you are); and the many friends and clients who have blessed my path with a word, a touch, a moment of your time.

Of the seven billion people on this planet (and counting) we have had the privilege to love, to grow and to know one another. It has been my deepest honor. I'm in awe of the universal love that exists for each of us worldwide. Words cannot begin to express my gratitude for the love, generosity and depth of intimacy I have shared with you all. My deepest love to all of you. May you continue to expand and experience how great-full we all really are. Blessings, blissings, kissings and love to your hearts. May you know the power of all-oneness and remember that love is always the reply to unleashing the beauty inside.

I could go on and on. Needless to say, I have many angels on my path who have supported me in innumerable and unconditional ways that are beyond generous and unexpected and gratefully received. I'm so privileged to have such a powerful team of men and women supporting this vision, opening hearts to stand in the truth of what we are. Love eternal.

INTRODUCTION TO TIFFANY SILVER

When I was a little girl I always wanted to marry a man whose last name was Gold. My brother had a best friend who was called Lucky Gold and I thought to myself, how I would just love to be Tiffany Silver Gold!

I didn't realize then how symbolic this would be for me later in life. The path was set and the quest begun, and I had no idea where it would take me.

As early as I can remember I was always curious and inquisitive. I loved to explore, I loved anthropology, I loved animals, but what fascinated me the most was the psychology of people. This led to a love of travel, as I unconsciously followed in my mother's footsteps. My mother has been traveling the world since I was an infant – once a year she and my father would visit another country for a month, and each time she would bring me back a doll from every place she visited. She also loved sharing the local cuisine, so we would be introduced to new dishes every time she came home.

At school, I had not been very popular; my brothers tortured me as I was growing up, and my only refuge was in being sick and staying home from school. I learned that this was how I got my needs met and where I could breathe freely for a few short hours without the disruption of pain or criticism.

I lived a very tumultuous life that brought me many experiences; I was adventurous, I didn't listen to authority and I pretty much beat my own drum. I had a knack at finding trouble, getting physically or emotionally hurt, encountering strange occurrences and people – I feel like I lived it all, "good and bad". I couldn't avoid pain – it seemed to follow me everywhere I turned.

My journey began at the age of 13, when I came of age in the Jewish tradition, the Bat Mitzvah, which celebrates the journey from girlhood to womanhood. But let me tell you, the last thing I felt like was a woman. I was not very feminine – I had zero curves! Anyways, back to the celebration! You are given a portion of The Torah (Old Testament) to recite in Hebrew in front of your family and peers. Mine was the story of Noah's Ark. (How appropriate, looking back! A man called Noah was required to become someone that no-one understood; regardless of the opinions of others, he forged ahead, knowing that even if you can't see the road ahead, you still pave the path.) The spiritual values of this lesson didn't resonate with me until now.

Studying Hebrew wasn't my favorite hobby, and instead of truly learning how to read each Hebrew character by sounding it out, I memorized the text at home on cassette (pre-CD days) and rehearsed it often, while pretending to read it. I was always looking for an easier way to do things; I just saw this as a better, more efficient distribution of time and energy. Think of it as a forced acceleration! How ironic; Noah had to work so hard building his ark – there was no short cut for his mission!

But I have found time and time again that the short cuts take as much energy as the long way round, as I have always been committed to knowing the truth, and being the best possible 'me'. Sometimes the short cuts turned into long journeys, and always at the back of my mind was the thought – never give up: even if it takes me a few years to catch up, I trust I am always right where I need to be.

Which takes me to today. I wrote this book four years ago, and had it edited three years ago by Gaynor Foster, whom I met while I was traveling in Australia. The book finally came into being, but it was shelved, as life got in the way. Finally, the time was right to resurrect it, and finish it. I was partly waiting for the title…and that of course was a journey in itself!

I met up with a former client I hadn't seen for a while, and over coffee, he casually gave me the title of this book! This miracle of Divine guidance spurred me to finish and publish the book you are now reading. In the midst of dental surgery and a lot of pain, I was able to call in everything I needed to bring this book to completion. What makes it more fun, interesting and exciting is that my book was first edited in Australia and then an Aussie friend who came to visit me this summer, bringing the journey full circle, designed the cover. My whole-world-family came together in this perfect moment to bring this book together!

Back to me at 13! After my Bat Mitzvah, my parents gifted my two brothers and I with a trip to Israel and Italy, two weeks in each country. It was on this trip that I would make two important distinctions that would shape the rest of my life, and lead me to my future. I went to the "Western Wailing Wall" in Jerusalem, where people from around the world gather to pray. The Wall, as it is known, is the last remnant of the Temple for the Jews in ancient times and is today considered a sacred site that holds the energy of antiquity, and is also a gateway and an anchor to G-d for the Jewish people to connect with, to experience their lineage.

Now, to this point I wouldn't have considered myself very spiritual; I don't even think I had formed or formulated a relationship with the creator and myself. However, on this day, at The Wall, I felt a presence of love, peace, and connection, like I was home. I felt connected to everything. In awe, I vowed that I would return and live there one day. This was my first awakening, and of course, it didn't last very long, and it would take many years to recapture that sense of love and unity again. That experience became an anchor for me, a beacon guiding me home.

After Israel came Italy; here I was, a 13-year-old blond, completely overwhelmed by the Italian male, and his attentions. I felt beauty in Italy, or more like beautiful, and I was drenched in the richness of food, art and culture. I felt the essence of being a woman everywhere I went. I loved it there, and decided I would live there one day. In Israel I felt G-d, and in Italy I felt my femininity and beauty – a great combo for a well-rounded recipe for life.

At the age of 15, almost 16, I was sent to military school in Roswell, New Mexico. (Talk about the antithesis of feminine!) This was a decision my father made in order to teach me discipline, to give me some boundaries, some rules and regulations, some structure. His intentions were good but at the time this was hardly the best way to nurture a sensitive, feminine young girl. Ironically, some 20 years later, I finally came to appreciate my experiences at this institute – this is when I truly saw that the divine mind had been operating in my life since my inception, and I saw the blessings that would come later in life from those two tortuous years. We were 100 women surrounded by 900 men; we were definitely in the minority and even though there was sexual tension and banter amongst us, we were not treated like queens, but more like servants, and this tainted my view of men and put paid to any ideas I had held that were equal.

I did survive and became the stronger for it, yet I seemed to be moving further from that feminine energy I so deeply desired to embody. Thankfully, my boyfriend in senior year really saved my life; I know he was an angel sent on my path to reveal what love was and is. (We were re-united 17 years later, the love between us still strong. I realized then that I'd spent my whole life looking for a man with his qualities. I experienced love for the first time with this man and this ignited the feminine in me, for a short time. He gave me hope, a spark of life, something to believe in. I had become increasingly unhealthier in both mind and body, and he provided a balm for my soul.)

I returned to Italy when I was 20, to finish my undergraduate degree in psychology, and I lived there for three years. I moved to California for a year, on a quest to find wholeness within myself, when I stumbled upon a Jewish meditation book; the moment I started reading it I knew I had to return to live and study and connect to my faith and to that presence I had felt when I was 13. The next day, my cousin called to invite me to a Sabbath meal the following Friday night at the home of a rabbi. It took just one conversation with that rabbi and three weeks later, I was on a plane bound for Jerusalem, to study Kabbalah.

I lived in Israel for four months studying with the orthodox Jews, living in the old city, and I also spent a month on the West Bank, studying The Torah at a yeshiva (a school just for women).

I knew nothing then about manifesting or creating my own reality; I had no idea my words had power and my subconscious thoughts could create as much as my conscious mind could. I knew one thing though – that I got what I wanted.

I spent many years searching for answers, thinking that something was wrong with me; I denied the feminine within, and I was constantly ill. I believed myself to be unlovable, as all my relationships were short-lived. Being vulnerable implied weakness, and clearly after living in a patriarchal household with two brothers and my father and then being shipped off to military school, my training in the softer, feminine aspect of myself was a bit skewed to say the least. I did however learn how to defend myself, to be a bully, to be assertive and yell! These qualities served me well in later life, but what I was really searching for was balance – and love. My core was gooey sweet and I could not deny that, try as I might. I was feminine but I hadn't the first clue about what that really meant, other than the fact I could use this to my advantage, sexually.

Outwardly I appeared feminine and soft, but inwardly my learned responses were geared toward defense, and sometimes offense. I learned that in order to get love I had to earn it – this is a very masculine model in our society, which values doing more than being. I was raised believing I had to earn my weight in gold. The alchemy of the feminine heart is the transformation I underwent during the last 15 years of my life. I must have hit the repeat button thousands of times over in order to pass each lesson, and these have become insights on how you can awaken to the authentic you which hides within.

If you want to wake up to your perception of reception, if you want to be flow, ease and love embodied, then this book is for you!

Come on this journey with me, so you may experience your own personal transformation of alchemy – the ability to transform base metals (your foundation) into the noble metals (your higher purpose of the heart) of gold or silver.

1

THE KEYS TO LOVING OPENLY

"Instead of 'I love you,' say, 'I am love'. The common expression is 'I love you.' But instead of 'I love you,' it would be better to say, 'I am love — I am the embodiment of pure love.' Remove the you, and I and you will find that there is only love. It is as if love is imprisoned between the I and you. Remove the I and you, for they are unreal; they are self-imposed walls that don't exist. The gulf between I and you is the ego.

When the ego is removed the distance disappears and the I and you also disappear. They merge to become one — and that is love. You lend the I and you their reality. Withdraw your support and they will disappear. Then you will realize, not that 'I love you,' but that 'I am that all-embracing love."

~Amma

Love from your being-ness, not your doing-ness. This is my story.

Inside of me was a belief that love should not have to be earned; that love is our birthright. It sounded good in theory...but the practice left much to be desired.

I found myself trapped in the need to deserve love.

When we're able to recognize the value and worth of our being simply because we exist, the need to do good, be good and act good becomes irrelevant.

When we don't recognize ourselves in this way, doing, being and acting 'good' in order to deserve love is an arduous, never-ending task. When you're clear that you're of value and worth, then you know that your ability to receive love is not based on your performance or how you behave.

For the most part, as infants we don't have to 'do' anything to receive love and attention. If you're here today as a walking, talking, functional two-legged being, then your caregivers took care of you. They provided food and shelter and, in order to give all of those necessities, touch was a part of the caregiving. In essence, the love of the universe provided a way for you to grow up in the most supported fashion possible.

(Of course, some babies do suffer neglect because what they need is not always apparent to the caregiver; and there are times when some caregivers can only do the minimum required to ensure the child's survival.)

As infants, you were not expected, nor were you able, to perform for high marks in order to receive love. You weren't doing handstands at one month old, saying, "Didn't I do well, now reward me, change my diaper and feed me!"

You were simply being. Love poured out of the universe wherever you were, to surround and engage with you. You knew the essence of your being and you delighted in discovering life, however it was presented to you. Without judgment or fear you stood witness to your creation as a manifestation in human form.

As adults, the love we seek has become based on reward and recognition. If I earn my way, if I demonstrate my worth and value, then I will be loved, I will be praised. In fact many of us thrive on these accolades – we wouldn't know what to do without them. This was my life, until 2009.

Who had I become?

As a healer, I had given away my life force for the love and approval of others, and the validation it brought when others transformed so quickly with my help. But I did it at great cost to myself.

I gave away my shine and left everyone else sparkling while I lay dried up and dusty, needing to go peel myself off the pavement. I was caught in repetitive cycles and if it hadn't been for the many healers who filled me back up after I'd empty everything I had onto my clients, I would have self-destructed.

I couldn't even see the pattern I was in. All I knew was that I loved to serve. I loved being able to help people attain their dreams in under five weeks. I prided myself on it. But I was dying inside. And fear was increasing. When I helped someone heal, they'd get everything they wanted, and I'd be left high and dry. I would go to every healer I could find and spend all the money I earned on healing, to get myself back to my shiny essence. It got so bad that in order to see any clients, I had to do sessions on myself every three days, and outsource to others two or three times a week. This was not my definition of thriving. I was surviving, disguised as love and light. I thought I was doing amazingly well, and in many ways I was, but at the same time, I lacked awareness of my pattern and I was constantly giving my power away.

I knew that in order to find myself again, I had to quit everything I knew that supported that life, and go cold turkey. I had to try a whole new way, with new people, new places and perhaps even a new career. I needed to find a place where I could make a difference, where I could use my talents, and not be consumed by them. A place where I could be loved for being me, not for what I did for others.

Sure, I had many moments of happiness. But I was always in fix-it mode, keeping my energy pristine, trying to be the best me I could be. But under all that was fear... a fear of not being loved and valued, and worse, a fear of picking up emotions and pain from others. This fear went so deep, that I wasn't able to see it. I just knew there was something wrong.

Part of this 'wrongness' manifested in an addiction to something that was extremely beneficial for others, but which in the end became toxic for me. I had become a machine junkie. I couldn't live without my biofeedback machine, because I never wanted to feel bad. I wanted to feel good all the time – the irony is that I abused this machine to such an extent that it stopped working for me and instead, it became the bane of my existence. It kept me in a state of perpetual fear – fear that if I didn't use it I would be so messed up I couldn't help anyone; and fear that if I didn't use it then people would really see that I was messed up.

Either way I had developed a very co-dependent relationship with my work device. In fact I had become so sensitive that I didn't feel comfortable hanging out with friends or going on dates for fear of the entities (energies) I saw in people's fields; for fear that these entities (energies) would hurt me. After being with other people, I would feel so bad and non-functioning, that I started to keep myself isolated. Anyone who wanted to spend any time with me was often told, sure I'll hang out with you – but can I clean up your energy first?

Not a great way to function! In fact I would often ask myself, how was I ever going to get married and have a normal life if I always had to fix people, because no one was ever really clear. This made my heart ache. I so desperately wanted to share love. I was becoming like my machine – a robot on autopilot; I had lost the ability to interact in a normal way. My whole identity was wrapped up in my ability to fix and change and improve your life that I didn't really have anything left for me, let alone anything left to share with another. The need to heal others had saturated my being and the fun was gone. I didn't really even know what fun meant.

When I look back, I can see the irony of it. I was helping everyone else, and doing a good job too! My machine was an amazing tool; when used with care and good intentions, it did amazing things for my clients. It did the same for me too in the beginning, but with the opposite result in the end. Through this device I discovered my own dysfunctions, masks and fears. I was afraid to be me, afraid to stand in my own power. So I hid behind the machine and let the machine take all the credit for my work; the machine became the validation of my existence. That became an addiction and when I wasn't able to maintain my existence without that constant life support, I knew that a change had to occur (or at least a change in perception).

I knew that I was fantastic at what I did with my clients, however I couldn't create what I really wanted for myself as I was hiding behind my fears; I was afraid to be great without something validating my greatness. It wasn't the machine that was bad – it was how I used the machine on myself that became the obsession. I was obsessed with feeling good, I was obsessed with healing the world, I was obsessed with proving that I was good enough over and over again. So enough was enough! I quit it all and I was terrified. How would I survive without my livelihood, without a machine that would tell me how well I was doing?

I removed myself from everyone in my life, starting over with the knowledge that this was a pivotal time for me. I began to deliberately create a plan, and that was to include new things that would support me in uncovering where I had gone astray, to see how I had ended up feeling so empty.

Help comes

I needed help, and I found it – I began to see a chiropractor Sai-Ling Michael once a month. More than a chiropractor – she was the next evolution of my being. She was (and is) a seer, a person who was able to do for me what I had done for so many. She was able to reveal my truth, showing me the patterns that kept me in survival mode. She helped me to step into my joy and be present to my body, my creations, and my motivations. She helped me to harness my psychic abilities by supporting me in being self-aware. She helped me to see and perceive patterns I carried with my parents that I constantly acted out with others. She aligned me to the truth of my being and showed me that I was a walking miracle.

In the beginning stages of this journey, I also saw another healer who opened my eyes to my fairy essence and being. He put me back in my body, right around the time of my 34th birthday. He measured my life force and said I was just a year shy of dying, that I had given away so much juice that there was barely anything left sustaining my vehicle. He did the repairs and I felt the best I had felt in years. It was like everything become crystal clear, bright and sparkly and I felt the power of my being and my feet on the ground for the first time in ages. But the problem was that he could not teach me to do it for myself. He could repair me, but it was up to me to stay happy and not give it all away.

That was a huge task! I wasn't used to keeping anything for me. But once I had discovered him, I wanted to feel this way all the time, so I went back for tune-ups once a week. He helped me tremendously, taking off all that otherworldly, inter-dimensional havoc I'd attract from leaving my body and not wanting to be with my feelings. I had learned to put up a 'vacant' sign in my hotel, and if I didn't direct what went in, then the space got filled anyways, and it wasn't usually with the energy I desired. The occupant was usually fear, or disconnection. Every healer I ever saw all said the same thing – that I was one of the most sensitive people they had ever met, and how could I function like this! Not very encouraging when you yourself don't know either!

This man helped me tremendously, but the problem was I didn't have the tools to do it for myself. I was left disempowered, because when I ran into a bind, if he didn't fix me or the machine didn't fix me, or if I didn't have someone there to get me back in my body, I would spin out. I would feel very suicidal at times, because I would lose perspective of what was true. Talking didn't help – I needed physical touch and spiritual manipulation and the grace of god to kiss me in order to awaken to my happy heart.

Needless to say my story with this man came to a close because I wasn't improving. I was just treading water, still full of fear of going out and interacting with others, because my sensitivities were running high. Fear still ran my life. I prayed and prayed and asked to be given tools, how could I teach the world **L**.iving **O**.penly **V**.ibrantly **E**.nergetically if I always ran to others to fix me?

In the midst of all this, I met another man Ed Japngie whose company develops products, which create neurological coherency in the brain. He believes that we are all under the effects of radiation from cell phone towers and the like. This man had invented an environmental conditioning tool that would limit the effects that these energies had on people. Brilliant! I was super impressed, in fact blown away by this! He developed solutions that when sprayed in the energy field would last up to six hours and would improve brain function, coordination and balance. But I also fell in love with another machine – the Merovector. All you had to do was plug this little box in and voila! The space got clear. It worked by helping me maintain a more positive attitude; it alleviated the effects of the things that kept me sluggish and in a brain fog.

I got clear and I felt grounded. I was excited to have this support, given my acute sensitivities, but I realized that no machine can take away the follies of the human heart; no machine can take away the necessity to tune in and see how you are feeling; and no machine can cut the cords to other humans and align you to your own heart's voice.

I had the best technology, the best healers, the best training in a million modalities, but I knew there was no magic pill. No one could help me to sustain a balanced life except me. I had become dependent on machines again, and I knew that this wasn't the way.

I found myself on a new journey of empowerment, and I had to do it alone.

No one could make me feel as good as when I could feel my true essence, and myself so nature became my best friend. I spent months in nature, praying, feeling and saying affirmations. I delighted in my childish ways. I delighted in the fact that I didn't need to fix anyone to feel good about myself. I delighted in my progress in life. I delighted in the potential that lay ahead. I spent time with friends doing simple things like sharing a meal and reveling in the awesomeness of life. I learned how to love myself and give to myself in ways I've never done before. I realized that self-care predicates good care for others. This had not been the case before, as I was in a gross imbalance in my life.

I gave myself time to be, time to experience my senses, time to trust and apply what I had been teaching others, time to awaken my sight and step into my power and realize my gifts. This was a time of awakening, clearing patterns and habits, identifying the source of origin of these behaviors, letting my energy shine and not giving it away for love and validation.

The Oneness Blessing

The other amazing and life-changing ally that came into my life at this time was the Oneness Blessing, also known as Desha, which catapulted me into love, acceptance and awareness. The Oneness Blessing is a neurobiological transfer of energy from Source that helps to close the parietal lobes, where all the mental chatter is, and open the frontal lobes, where peace resides.

The Deeksha (gift of grace) awakens the heart to its purest form. I came to experience this benediction over two years ago and I thought I had found the Holy Grail! Well, in one aspect it was that for me, because it did create these brain shifts.

After coming into contact with the Oneness Blessing, I experienced three months of bliss. I discovered that I was amazing – not because my clients told me, or because my parents encouraged and approved of me – I discovered it by being with myself, by observing the simple beauty all around me. I saw humanity and divinity coursing through everyone I encountered, and I celebrated the contrast life presented. I embraced my fears and I stopped judging my process. I stopped resisting the pain and just let everything rise to the surface. I paid attention to it all and denied nothing. I went with the flow and I allowed for the unknown. I allowed myself to discover me, through the actions and reflections of others. I saw them as mirrors of myself.

I surrendered to letting love in, and I stopped beating myself up for all that I hadn't accomplished. I celebrated the Law of Attraction and I celebrated the people who were currently choosing to participate in my journey. I was awe-inspired moment to moment, trusting that god was my supply and that all my needs were taken care of.

After three months of deep introspection I came to conclude that I loved helping people. I want to uplift, inspire and teach L.O.V.E., not because I had an obligation to do so, or because I owed it to god or anyone else. I was choosing to do it because it satisfies my soul to its very core. My being loves to love; in fact I live for love, nothing makes me happier. Since I learned what self-serve means, I realize I am here to serve myself joy! And what brings me the most joy is sharing my discoveries and gifts.

So when I discovered that I wanted to continue pursuing my healing practice I was both amazed and relieved. As well as wanting to continue helping others, my goal and vision was to spread this love to as many people as possible, through the media, so the need to write this book arose.

This book is a tangible manifestation of my life, and my gifts, that I can share with others. I also realized that now that I had come up with a formula for empowering lives and for being one's own healer that I would like to demonstrate it on TV…

I was ready for an agent to make this happen, and the one thing I know is that when you get crystal clear and you align your energies, miracles happen. I called up an agent I had met three months earlier. I wasn't ready for him then, but now I was! So we met a few days later, and I demonstrated my gifts to him. I began to channel flow and share from my heart, incorporating all my different modalities. After a few hours he was raw, revealed and uncovered. He discovered many truths he had been blind to, as to why he was the way he was. He could see what was stopping him from attaining the next level of his success, and he discovered the need to be more loving of himself and the need to take better care of his physical body.

We were both super excited about our meeting, and I felt centered, happy and confident that my dreams were manifesting step-by-step. Well, this happened on a Friday and I called him the following Monday to check in on him, to see how the treatment had settled in. He told me he felt good, that he was aware of a shift and that he was experiencing a lot of new awarenesses. I felt pleased, so I asked him, now that he had seen and experienced my work, would he represent me so I could share this on a TV show, worldwide.

He told me he was willing to see if there was an open audience, but he was still trapped in his skepticism and started reeling off all the obstacles that might present themselves. I stopped him in his tracks and said – I know what you've been accustomed to, and what you've experienced, but I'm here to show you a new way. I'm here to break the old paradigms of how we think things need to occur to get what we want. He agreed! Underneath all that skepticism lay a true optimist.

He promised to give me an opportunity, but warned me that it would be one shot only, and I had better be prepared! He called me the next day, and said: "We're on!" He had set up a meeting with a TV show on a major network that was looking for a life coach. He was very impressed with my ability to manifest!

Wow, was my universe fast! Of course, it all made sense; I had given myself three months off because I was preparing for this…ah, I felt confident and giddy. So off to the audition I went and they loved me so much I became friends with the casting director. I made it to the last round, but they had really been looking for someone with a PhD, and not so spiritual! I later found that they had selected two girls, one in New York and one in Chicago, but the project didn't go ahead. I realized that something better must be coming, and in the meantime my agent and I got closer, and he watched in amazement my power of intention. I had just read 'The Game of Life and How to Play It' by Florence Scovel Shinn, and in it she says: "god makes a way where there is no way". So I told my agent to repeat this and make a call to the producer of the TV show, rather than email him. He trusted my guidance and I prayed and repeated this mantra: god makes a way where there is no way. Let this be for the highest good of all concerned, align me to my highest path. He called me back in amazement! He said, "Okay, Tiffany, you got a second chance! I can't believe this stuff really works!"

We set a date to meet, for a time when things had slowed down for the producer. I was pleased and yet I was still trying to find my footing, and this was the closest I ever came to landing a show. I thought I was ready, but I didn't realize there were still lessons to be learned before I was really ready to get out there and teach the world! I still had unresolved issues with my father.

During the three months of being-ness, my father and I didn't speak. I didn't call because I didn't want to tell him I was living on faith and my credit cards, and he didn't call because he didn't want to hear that I wasn't working. So we were both happy in our unspoken communication until I came to realize that I didn't call because I was afraid he would reject me and reprimand me. I was afraid he would be mad at me for screwing around for three months while he worked his "ass off" according to his value system, using his words. I didn't want the guilt or the judgment, because I knew he could never understand what I was doing. If I hadn't taken this time to reinvent myself, I wasn't sure that I would have survived. His very conventional, conservative mind would not let him understand how I could be incapacitated energetically; this was unfathomable to him. He understood order, structure and discipline, and how would I make a living if I wasn't working, if I was just sitting around? He came to understand later that I was 'training'; it was almost as if I had gone to get my PhD and all my attention was on my studies. I thought I would call him when the TV show was booked and confess then...telling him, "see, aren't I great, look what I did! I honored myself and took time to learn, I honed my craft and now I'm on a national TV show and money is about to come in big!" Well, that didn't happen – in fact just the opposite did! I had to call him and tell him of my defeat and ask him for a loan because things hadn't gone as planned. To my surprise, he was quite impressed with my progress. In fact I think it was the first time that he saw that what I was doing wasn't just a bunch of fluff, but that I had really mastered something for a larger audience.

My experience in auditioning brought new lessons. I needed to become even more integrated and shift my language to appeal to a larger audience. There were still refinements to make before I could truly step up and teach and still more fears to be faced, particularly with my father.

He didn't call me because he feared I wouldn't succeed and he'd have to give me money, and I was afraid that if I called I wouldn't succeed and he'd have to give me money! A self-fulfilling prophecy if ever there was one! I needed to face my fear in order to have a new approach to my relationship with my father; I needed to see where that fear had come from. When he agreed to give me some money, I made one stipulation – he had to give it to me anticipating my success, not fearing that I would fall on my ass again. He needed to know that this wasn't going to be a litany of endless financial requests. He had already hinted at this, saying, "well, what if you need money in another month, and what if you can't get it together?" I told him that I would rather not receive his contribution if it was tied to lack, fear and failure, that I would only accept this money because he supported my PhD (or my PhD, as my best friend calls it – god's honorary degree). This was a demonstration of empowerment for me, and I realized from this point forward that I always wanted to be honest with my father. I wanted to share my life with him, even if it made him feel helpless. I wanted his moral support more than his financial support. So we agreed, and I have been prosperous ever since, and that fear has been extinguished.

New fears arise now concerning emotions, and I am certain that as my fears percolate to the surface, they will be purged and I will have a cleaner slate to create from. Bring it on, let me be free! Let me free myself of unwanted fears that block me from receiving and perceiving my joy and happily creating my heart's desires! May I continue to refine my ways and be a person whose highest concern is to accept and get along and acknowledge my humanity and my needs, and find fulfilling ways to meet those needs.

How to set yourself free

1. Feel yourself in love

Let the heart navigate your route! The only way to be in love is to see and feel yourself in love. I've never known anyone who has ever truly felt love and called it by any other name. Love is a 'whole being' experience; it does not only exist in the heart but it consumes your entire being; it emanates from your aura; it's a way of living in love, not just a happening, but a state of eternal being once you've made the choice to be dedicated to love above all else.

This may mean you make sacrifices for love or you let someone win an argument for the sake of maintaining love. If love is your destination, may no man put asunder your plan. Love will command how you direct your choices. Love will help you reset in times of fear and pain. Love will give you the motivation and inspiration to forge forward. If love is at the crux of it all, then your life will take on a new meaning. Perhaps the way you once interacted will change and you may soften your tone or your demeanor or your manner. Love will guide and lead you. If you are hanging on to regret, anger or resentment, love may melt it all away and lead you toward what it is you really want to feel. If you're willing to self examine and dedicate your life to L.O.V.E., you'll find that the struggle ends. It's almost like becoming a saint because your main aspiration is to fulfill being loving to yourself and others through acts of forgiveness, allowance and acceptance, surrender and celebration. And in the end you will embrace what life brings to you and find the silver lining in it all.

Love can be your new compass in life; your soul's dedication. If I am dedicated to love, to giving and receiving, then I remain open to infinite possibilities and I am honest with what I know to be my truth. I understand there are no absolutes in life and that I remain flexible and eager to realize my true nature, and be all that I can be. I let life be an array of beautiful choices and I say yes to that which supports the realizations of my heart's desires. I recognize everyone and everything upon my path as a valuable player and even if it hurts, there is something I can learn from each and every interaction. Every day I use my experiences to determine the things that align with my higher self. I lean towards that which promotes the upliftment of my being. I stand in gratitude for all exchanges and I know that I have free will to make choices. I choose to be loving rather than be right.

2. Command, not demand!

You don't need others to empower you in your truth. I spent my whole life demanding what I wanted and that led to a lot of resistance and pain. I found that changing my tone and empowering the way I asked for what I wanted allowed me to manifest everything I needed. I found that if I commanded my life, it meant taking charge of my assertions, while not pushing my assertions on others.

A leader commands his troops to victory, he does not demand it; he leads the way powerfully by example, strength, awareness and confidence. Commanding your life is about becoming the leader in the direction you will take next. It requires you to be the driver, to steer your route with eyes open, not be the passenger yelling and screaming at the driver to do it your way! If you want it your way, then command your vehicle towards the destination of your desires. It's the *Ten Commandments*, not the ten *demandings*…these are powerful instructions for how to live your life. There is no force involved, just choice – but the word commandment implies a direction of power and fortitude. So follow your commandments and trust they are summonings of god to your highest destination on your journey.

3. Ask yourself: do you want the experience?

Experience is the only reason to ever want to participate in anything. I used to struggle with making decisions and sometimes the deciding factor was: do I have the finances to support the choice being presented? I got really tired of making decisions based on my economic status; one day I realized any time I ever really wanted to do something, nothing stood in my way. I didn't have to fixate on the dollar because I was certain of the destination. When I've decided to do something and truly based my decision upon wanting the experience, the experience appears! Magical events will align themselves with your desire every time. So I realized that it's never about the money, and that goes for all things in life. When invited to a party or a meeting with a friend, a trip, a walk, a hike, I ask myself: "do I want this experience?" If my answer is yes, then god will make it happen. And I eagerly prepare for my next experience based on the desire to have that encounter. If I am not 100 per cent sure, and a huge financial commitment is pending, then more often than not the situation will not come to pass, because there was no passion for the event in the first place. Perhaps that was my guidance leading me in another direction by not supplying the money, because I was meant to be right where I was.

THE KEYS TO LOVING OPENLY | 33

Follow your heart and ask yourself always, do I want this experience? This can alleviate a lot of pain and any sense of obligation to another, because if you realize you don't want the experience, you may have the courage to say no, and do what it is you really want to do. It makes life so much more fulfilling because when you realize you do things because you want to, then showing up becomes exciting, fun and playful.

As an example of this: I began working with my biofeedback system and was loving every moment of it. I thirsted for more every day. In the first two months of being exposed to this advanced bio-feedback technology I was super impressed and clients were eager to try it, and I was so enthusiastic that I ended up selling 4 machines in two months! I was completely aligned with demonstrating my faith and getting results. Not only did I get results but the proof was in the pudding, because I was thousands of dollars richer, and ferocious for more! And so the opportunities kept arriving. One day I was thinking how I'd love to go back to visit Italy again. I had lived there for three years and I felt like it would be an opportune time to go again. It just happened that the advanced training for my bio-feedback was being offered in Budapest, Hungary – right next door! So I sent out my rocket of desire (as Abraham, channeled by Esther Hicks, would call it) and a few days later I got a long distance client in Italy with whom I started working weekly.

After a few sessions I mentioned the idea of visiting and doing some work in person and she thought it was a fabulous idea and offered me a guesthouse in Florence to work from for the summer. She would also start drumming up business for me. So within no time not only was I going to Italy, I had a job there, and I was going to Hungary to do my training. I wasn't concerned about money; I just knew what I wanted and all the money and resources made them available to me.

Similarly, when I first experienced the Oneness Blessing, I knew I had to go to India to become a Oneness Blessing giver. Shortly after, I met Annette Carlstrom, who is a leading light in this organization, and then Sri Anandagiri-ji, then senior disciple to the founders of Oneness University in India.

I had prayed for the next phase in my evolution; I wanted to arrive at peace and serenity once and for all. From what I had seen in Annette and Anandagiri-ji, this seemed like the ticket. I then received a call from Oneness University, inviting me to attend a private course; they had heard how passionate I was about the Blessing and wanted me to become a Blessing Giver myself.

I knew that this would be a life-changing decision, but two weeks before the course was due to start, I still didn't have the money to go. I wanted the experience, though! I asked spirit, if this is for my highest good then let it come with ease and grace – and it did! I made $4,600, bought my ticket the week before I flew out, and got my visa and a new passport as well. This was a mission from god, and I had to be there. So you see the money never gets in the way if your commitment is strong.

4. Willingness

Resign your resistance and open up to willingness.

Resistance is the number one key that will prevent you from graduating from lesson to lesson. Resistance may even be the thing that keeps you locked and bound in the repetition of your story. In order to grow and have all you desire, you must be willing to learn; you must be willing to forgive; you must be willing to try new things; you must be willing to be uncomfortable; you must be willing to be embarrassed; you must be willing to make an ass out of yourself; you must be willing to be hurt; you must be willing to succeed, and be willing to fail.

Your willingness will allow you the wherewithal to know what's next on your path. Be willing and willingness will find you and surround you. Meet your resistance and resistance will fall away and what you will encounter will be surrender and a graciousness to experience life. You'll experience people eager, ready and willing to help you. Be willing and when you recognize your resistance to accepting what is, or to doing something new that makes you uncomfortable – be still. Breathe into your heart and see if the willingness comes. If the resistance is your block, due to pride and ego, do nothing until you can sort out the real motivation behind your resistance. Check in to see if what you're resisting is worth it. If you're committed to living a life that inspires; a life filled with love; a life of celebration, then you may just do nothing until right action makes itself clear to you. Listen with an open heart – you will be guided.

I equate resistance with ego. Everything I resist is usually because my mind believes that this isn't really how things ought to be; or because I set my intentions for something else and look at how awful it's showing up! In that moment of resistance I am not willing to adapt to my present circumstance and make the best out of it, in fact I am often selfish and needing my immediate needs met, and definitely not acting in accordance with being loving and inspiring. I am acting instead out of self-fulfilling motives in order to not feel uncomfortable.

Sometimes the best thing to do is agree, surrender and walk away in high esteem. Resisting unexpected circumstances and trying to hold a position of inflexibility will only lead to opposition. Remember your commitment is to be good to yourself above all, and if forcing a situation to occur might oppose another's position, then it's up to you to walk away, surrender or make space for right action. I firmly believe that we only want to be where we are wanted, so forcing someone to love you or treat you lovingly when they don't feel that, will only hurt you. If you can stay true to you, and loving you, then you will not need to oppose another; you will be able to respect what they ask, as long as it doesn't compromise the integrity of who you are. You cannot force another to love you the way you see fit, especially if they don't have the capacity to love themselves in the same way. If you want someone to tend to you in a nurturing, caring and honoring way, look to see if they do this with themselves. This will be a valuable indicator to let you know if you're asking someone to be other than who they really are.

We all have the ability for love, tenderness and affection, but not everyone has been raised to feel comfortable in expressing their true Divine nature; many need to hold on to control and boundaries in order to feel safe. Learn to observe people in their own terrain and you will be better equipped to meet them where they're at.

There is a beauty in avoidance, because whatever it is that you're not wanting will be the very thing to come and annoy you! Ironic – or should we call it by its real name, Law of Attraction! You don't want certain things to happen; for example, you avoid interacting with people in order to avoid conflict, but the conflict is waiting for you and if it doesn't show up as a direct correlation to the situation you are avoiding, it will show up somewhere else.

Resistance, avoidance and neglect give you the opportunity to grow and ultimately allow you to make peace with what scares you the most. You may find that it's never as bad as you thought or imagined. If you don't confront the thing that keeps you separate, it will continually show up over and over again. Each time will be a new story describing the same thing. All of this resistance and avoidance is a by-product of fear – fear of telling the truth; fear of being hurt, or of hurting someone, a fear of being disempowered, or a fear of moving forward. All of the things we avoid will come to bite us in the ass later, so if you know what you're avoiding or fearful of, ask spirit to bring you the lesson you need in a timely manner, and stay in gratitude. What you fear or resist will continually present itself in order to be healed, so that you can move on, and go out into the world freely, eagerly awaiting all things.

5. Make yourself Number One

Be the lighthouse – let the ships sail into you. Some people naturally do this, they are attractors and all that they have just comes to them – they aren't even aware of how fortunate they are. They step into the world full of confidence and the world is at their feet to serve. It's an attitude, not an action. They're not seeking, they are the sought after; they exude a confidence that people are attracted to. They feel their power and they show up and know that whatever it is they are wanting will be there in some way. This isn't to say that people who have it all don't want more or in different ways, but they never struggle with the idea of loss. In fact the opposite applies. These people are always creating more for themselves.

In order to care for others and share effectively, you must care for yourself first. There's a difference between a person who is self-ish and a person who seeks self-fulfillment. Which one are you? A selfish person does not like to share and is motivated by taking whatever they can get in life. A person who is self-fulfilling knows that in order to attain happiness they must do things for themselves first, in order to share later. They know that in order to give they must have something to share, and so they fulfill their needs in order to give more later.

Self-fulfilling people maintain their vehicle in order to share from the overflow; they never tap into their savings and give from a depleted place. How do you move from selfish to self-fulfilling?

Ask yourself: "Why do I come from a place of selfishness? What has caused me to focus on myself, and ignore the other?"

Perhaps in the past you gave and got depleted. There is something to be learned, in your over-giving. Perhaps you over-gave because you wanted love and approval or you wanted to prove your worth. If you don't want to share, and you are forced by circumstances to do just that, what you need to realize is – as a human being on this planet, whatever you don't want to do will be presented to you until you've understood the lesson.

6. Faith in self produces faith in others

This theory applies to all things in life. If you want people to believe in you, you have to believe in yourself. Since we are all just emotion (energy in motion), we are always giving off signals and we don't have to speak to communicate. That's why it's important to focus on what we want, rather than what we don't want.

If you're just a walking, talking signal, then being in vibration with what you're asking for in life is a 24-hour a day process. It doesn't just stop once you enter into your cocoon at night. You are always downloading information from source, and source is reaching into the minds of all to orchestrate the next happening, to create the manifestation of your focus and attention. You'd be amazed at how many things you can create when you start paying attention to your thoughts. The more we become what we want others to see in us, the more others will see what we believe about ourselves. Growing up, it always amazed me how others could read me and see who I was, before I even knew who I was! They could see the things that blocked me from becoming who I wanted to be. No one could have sped up the process for me, despite all my awareness and insights. We are all on our own time line and in order to truly become who we know ourselves to be, we have to play certain stories out.

These stories will stop repeating themselves when we are truly ready to make our mark in life. It takes courage to move on, it takes courage to believe in ourselves despite who we've been. It takes patience and resilience to evolve into remembering our magnificent selves, but we can take it one day at a time. This book has been written to encourage you to do whatever it takes to practice self-awareness and dedicate yourself to love above all. And that means loving yourself first. Feel the love within you. No one can ever make you happy; they can only accentuate the feeling you already have inside of you. They can't take away your inner strife and struggle – only you can reconcile that within you. So remember, if everything is vibration, what vibe are you giving out? If you're giving out a vibe that does not feel good to you, then think of how others may feel around that vibe. Tune in and tune up your vibe to the frequency of your choices. Get clear. Focus. Visualize. Faith is the act of believing that infinite possibilities are available to everyone you meet.

7. Know your destination

The key to life is: know your destination, and be willing to change paths to get there. Know where you're going, and where you've come from. All you have is this moment NOW, this moment when you can readjust the dial on your radio and tune into to any station you like. If you don't like what you hear, change the channel. Life is about constantly knowing when to tune the dial to a station that better suits your needs. You may find that you like to adjust things daily or you may find that you are as loyal as they come and you harmonies just fine on one particular path. There is no wrong way – but remember that it isn't just about the destination; it's the journey along the way. Stop and breathe in those precious moments and if you don't like the story of your past, resolve to change it and write yourself a new script.

You may have to shoot the same scene over and over again, but there is beauty in knowing when you're done with a particular scene. And there'll be another to enact very soon! In the meantime enjoy being replete, enjoy the transition, enjoy the not knowing and if you get hung up in Groundhog Day, know that all you have to do is decide to do something different – and move! Move forwards, sideways, backwards, anyway! Just move. Movement can create new pathways of exploration, and what seemed like a mundane existence suddenly gets colorful with new life and a change of scenery.

8. When something closes it becomes your opening

I've wanted to deny this theory for years, but just when I believe that it can't be true, I get more evidence that it is! When a door closes, it is always reopened with something more excellent, but you may not be able to see it at the time. Sometimes when I look back I'm able to find the blessings in disguise, but I guarantee that when life closes a relationship or opportunity, something new is coming. The best you can do is happily anticipating the next momentous thing as an opportunity to align more with who you are remembering yourself to be.

9. Home is where the heart is

So many people think that if they just relocated, their life would get better. If they ran away and started over, then life could be good. I spent my whole life running away, moving from country to country and State to State, but I could never escape what was within me. I could mask certain symptoms and patterns but at the end of the day, my home was not about where in the world I was located – my home was when I decided to feel good inside my heart wherever I was.

And that was only possible when I started to address the issues that kept me running in the first place. Running away never made my problems go away – it just postponed the inevitable confrontation within myself. Step into your heart to see and feel into the truth of your reality. From this place you can set yourself free and reset into possibility.

10. Clean out your space in order to love

Clear the clutter, organize your life, and place things deliberately on your path – these will inspire your movement forward. Life presents many ways to display who you are but we can become inundated with remnants of the past. The clearer the space that you live in, the more you can create. Clutter is subjective, I know, but when you're surrounded by a past that no longer represents the real you, you need to eliminate the clutter and step into the moment and your unfolding presence. Since my storage are my stories, reminiscing has its benefits, however it depends upon the associations you have to those objects – every object holds a story and energy. You'll know when you're ready to let go to make that courageous pass forward, and if letting go is a challenge, have a friend help you, as they can see from a broader view what may be inundating you.

I found that I was holding onto so many things from my past because they represented security and a place of comfort, but when I lifted myself free of the memories of my past, I lifted the weight those memories held in my consciousness and I freed my mind to focus on aligning myself with my future creations. I have since become a minimalist; the less I have to manage, the more energy I have for other things in my life. Every day my desire is to eliminate clutter, to free myself of attachment and to make room for new objects of my desires. Making room for the new only happens when we empty out the old.

We can't ever go looking for something new when we've become complacent with what we have. Comfort even in an uncomfortable situation is harder to leave for the unknown, due to fear of change and fear of getting less than you already have. In order to remedy this you must make courageous passes toward attaining the next goal. To do this, you have to leave behind the mediocre...and step into the unknown with anticipation of excellence.

CHAPTER ONE SUMMARY:
THE KEYS TO LOVING OPENLY

"Love from your being-ness, not your doing-ness".

How to set yourself free:

1. Feel yourself in love. Love can be your new compass in life, your soul's dedication.

2. Command not demand! The word commandment implies a direction of power and fortitude. Follow your commandments and trust they are summonings of god to your highest destination on your journey.

3. Ask yourself: do you want the experience?

4. Willingness: Resistance keeps you in the story of your limitations; willingness opens the field of possibilities. There is a beauty in avoidance, because whatever it is that you're not wanting will be the very thing to come and annoy you! What you fear or resist will continually present itself in order to be healed, so that you can move on.

5. Make yourself Number One: Be the lighthouse – let the ships sail into you. In order to care for others and share effectively, you must care for yourself first. There's a difference between a person who is self-ish and a person who seeks self-fulfillment.

6. Faith in self produces faith in others: Since we are all just emotion (energy in motion), we are always giving off signals and we don't have to speak to communicate. That's why it's important to focus on what we want, rather than what we don't want.

7. Know your destination: All you have is this moment NOW, this moment when you can readjust the dial on your radio and tune into to any station you like. If you don't like what you hear, change the channel. There is no wrong way – but remember that it isn't just about the destination; it's the journey along the way. Stop and breathe in those precious moments and if you don't like the story of your past, resolve to change it and write yourself a new script.

8. When something closes it becomes your opening: When a door closes, it is always reopened with something more excellent, but you may not be able to see it at the time.

9. Home is where the heart is: Home is not about where in the world you are located – home is when you decide to feel good inside your heart wherever you are.

10. Clean out your space in order to love: Making room for the new only happens when we empty out the old. We can't ever go looking for something new when we've become complacent with what we have. Leave behind the mediocre...and step into the unknown with anticipation of excellence.

2

NO MISTAKES: Humanity vs. Divinity

"See God in every person, place, and thing, and all will be well in your world."

~Louise L. Hay

"People who love themselves come across as very loving, generous and kind; they express their self-confidence through humility, forgiveness and inclusiveness."

~Sanaya Roman

There are no miss-takes in life.

The most common thing I hear is: I made a mistake; he made a mistake. What does that really mean, to mis-take life? It shouldn't have happened? You didn't get it right? That assumes there is a right way for life to unfold.

If we were solving math, yes, then there is a right and wrong answer and, usually, 2+2 will equal 4, not 5 or 6. But life isn't like math, and there isn't just one result or way of doing something. Those who believe in a universe that obeys the law of grace would argue that mistakes don't exist – only learning occurs – and in order to learn you have to experience life in its contrast. Therefore mistakes are impossible.

You may not get the result you were looking for, but that doesn't make it a mistake. You may have miscalculated, but can you call it a mistake? Yes, you can definitely get a different result, but that's no reason to beat yourself up. Why not live in a world that adheres to a different philosophy – one where you do your best and, given all the variables and circumstances, you make allowances for improvement? Your whole life would change if you stopped believing you messed up, and started believing instead in your invincible nature, which is to learn and grow as you progress. Only by mis-taking life for what you thought was the right outcome do you learn how to adjust to what suits all concerned.

The learning occurs in those mis-taken moments because that is where you extract deeper insights into what has happened. From this place of seeing with awareness, what would you have done differently? Utilize this as a marker for the future. There may be moments you forget to apply the insights you've acquired, however the knowledge is now there and the opportunities are certain to arise for another chance to do it over.

There is a natural order to how life moves forward. When there is a contrast between what you are choosing and what is occurring, watch for the lesson! Problems come when you believe you've made a mistake; you start making excuses as to why you did what you did, you start justifying and explaining, and this perpetuates the victim/perpetrator mentality.

Every situation offers the opportunity for you to re-evaluate why you're holding to a limited belief system. If you remove the idea of 'mistakes' from your life, then life becomes a place in which to grow and learn. If you don't have the 'correct' answer at least you've made an effort to find a solution, and in making the effort, growth occurs. If we didn't try, then no growth is possible, and life would grind to a halt...which is not possible! It is in the contrast that we grow; it is from the perceived 'mistakes' that we learn. So learn from the 'mistakes' and then move forward with forgiveness and awareness, with the understanding that life will always present another opportunity or rematch! And it won't always be with the same person or situation, but it will be another opportunity to see how well you can 'go with the flow'.

If along the way, Life determines that you need to repeat a particular lesson (and one you thought you had learned!) then clearly there was another layer beneath the surface that you didn't address, and that would have a direct benefit for you. Life will find a way to orchestrate events to refine the process and make you the best person you can be incrementally, as you move into the divinity in all things. It helps to remember that we are all doing our best and it also helps to see that there is Divine action behind everything. Forgive yourself and others and embrace the wisdom of every situation as it rises, and see it as an opportunity to become a more whole person.

Forgiving is the act of for-giving, for-sharing and for-caring. When we are not in the act of for-sharing, we are in self-fulfillment, and that may not give us the foresight to know how to pay attention to the needs of others and their personal comfort. If there is no such thing as a miss-take, just learning and growth, then no forgiveness is necessary or possible. How can we forgive someone who is learning? Why would we need to forgive people for their process of growth?

However if you are engaging with people who still believe in the model of victim-perpetrator, then this is an act of compassion, recognizing that they have not come into a self realized position in life where apologies are no longer necessary.

If you are mean to someone, apologize. An apology acknowledges that pain has occurred as a direct result of your actions, deliberate or not. We all say and do things we may regret later, not understanding ourselves well enough in the moment to really know why we did what we did. When this happens, know that you have come from a place of hurt, a place of defense, and a place of protection

I encourage forgiveness because it's not an admission that what you did or how you did it was wrong – it's about acknowledging that you may have participated as the catalyst that caused feelings of pain and sorrow in another. If you ask me, how can I forgive a man who beats his wife or a man who molests children, I will ask you – how can I not? Clearly a person of this nature is filled with so much self-hate and pain that they know no other way to express their agony than to act out on others. If you don't know how to handle your own pain, if you have not been equipped with the tools for life, how can we expect you to be an upstanding individual? I believe that no man was born to be evil, and that evil occurs through loss of love, because we have lost our connection to the Divine.

When we begrudge another for not behaving in a way that suits us, the only person this anger, frustration and resentment hurts is ourselves. When we hold people to an expectation to be different from whom they are, we only hurt ourselves. The act of forgiveness is to free you from the pain you create from desiring others to be different from who they are.

I would love to see a world full of loving, clear communicating, sharing and caring individuals, but in order to create that as my reality, I must be that myself. I cannot expect others to be what I am not and I cannot expect that others will ever understand why being loving may create a happier life. But what I can do is have compassion for the learning curve and, most of all, be for-giving to myself along the way for my perceived mis-takes. Once you forgive people for your expectations of them, and how they should be so that you can be more comfortable, you can then make way for becoming that person yourself! They can remain as they are, as you accept what is and free yourself of the energy it takes to harbor resentment towards people and their actions.

People can become paralyzed in their responses and may not act according to your timing. If we are experiencing a situation, then we are co-creating it; like it or not, both parties are coming fully loaded with stories of how to respond to certain behaviors. So, more likely than not, if you are holding a pattern unresolved, you will encounter the person who will bring light for this pattern to surface to be healed.

You may be unaware that this pattern or program was even in your system, so thank that person for revealing this opportunity to see the layers deeper within the self, layers that prevent us from being loving and co-operative and compassionate. We really all come so fully loaded with our own agenda; we receive love the way we give love and anything outside our perception can lead to separation and judgment. The choice is always available to you, do you want to be loving, or do you want to be right?

Can you see it from their point of view? It's not up to us to determine if what that person is expressing is right or wrong or even merits our time and attention, because whatever shows up is real for that individual, and they deserve to be acknowledged for their experience. Compassion will allow you to humble yourself to see it from their perspective. It helps you to see that we selfishly want to impose our ideas onto the other as appropriate for them. Appropriate is subjective to your ability to flow with the higher wisdom that know no laws or rules and is ever-flowing in the arms of grace.

Here's an exercise that was given to me by Dr. Sai-Ling Michael – this is my adaptation of it. For one week conjure all the people, places and situations that you perceive have created harm in your life and left you feeling hurt or resentful. Put them into your heart. "By placing people in your heart they no longer have power over you because they reside in the most sacred part of you." Then imagine you have a large washing machine and place one person at a time inside, then add your genuine forgiveness to the mix. Holding onto the pain is only hurting you and in order to move forward and receive a new outcome you have to let go of the past and start anew. Wash these individuals around in your heart; find the common denominator between you and them – find their divinity, forgive their humanity, step into their shoes for a minute and have compassion for their inability to be what you needed them to be.

One by one, release them down a grounding cord of light, which acts as a funnel into the earth, and allow the earth to absorb all the past hurts and pains and expectations or embarrassment. (Chapter 4 covers this in more depth.)

Remember, most of the time the person we really need to forgive is ourselves for having been enrolled in these painful interactions.

Do this for a week on a daily basis and you'll be surprised how many people from your past may be inside. I discovered that I needed to forgive my 5th Grade teacher for saying in front of the classroom: "Tiffany woke up on the wrong side of the bed, and there was only one side to wake up on!" This stayed with me my whole life and was just one more validation of my unworthiness. I carried the hurt and embarrassment for a long time. Now I'm positive that this teacher made these comments without realizing the impact they would have on me...but this is life. We are constantly storing and filing what others say, to either confirm a belief about whom we think we are or to confirm what others think we are. So dig deep into the archives of your mind and discover what may still be lingering that supports an attitude of pain in your present life. This is an excellent way to see just where you're really at and if what you're harboring even has validity anymore.

In understanding the Laws of Attraction, I now have more compassion for what I created in the past. I continually recreated the same situations throughout my life and tried to blame others for my pain. No matter where I went, the lessons followed me, and I ultimately had to take responsibility for all I had created, and forgive them all – because they had just became a player in my script. Forgive all and free yourself of the expectation that people are responsible for how you think and feel.

Create, don't dictate

Dictating how your life needs to be just creates great strain and expectation on those around you. Life is to be felt and created from moment to moment, so when you're demanding or dictating how things ought to be, you may be missing out on an authentic life, and you may overlook the beauty that can bring.

Have you ever met someone who you thought was a certain way, and you pegged them in a hole from a quick first impression, judging them by the friends they hang out with? You now start to react to this person from these judgments; never really giving them a fair chance because you were seeing through your own filter of how you thought this person would fit into your life. All the while you're missing out on who and what this person really is because you've refused to allow them to be other than your opinion of them. So you don't share your life with this person, and all their talents go undiscovered because you assumed they were something they are not. You've now begun to demand and dictate to a perfect stranger, and you're asking them to be and act and do things that may not suit them, and because you have a blind spot you cannot see what it is you are really working with. Dictation and demanding is a waste of the potential for co-creation that you both have. Take a moment to tune in to the humanity of everyone who is choosing to serve you or participate with you. You may discover that your robotic, entitled ways are ungrateful and you could choose to stop long enough to really be present and perhaps discover something more inside of them. At the same time, you will discover something in yourself as well. If you adhere to the theory that all you ever experience is yourself, then every person holds a piece of the puzzle, something for you to discover in order to see the bigger picture in completion.

How to lighten up, have fun in your life, and let go

I had a client who never tried for anything in life. When he was in his teens his mother became ill, and he made the decision that he was no longer allowed to enjoy life because his mom was suffering; he never wanted to bring her more pain by being happier than her, so he stopped enjoying life. He just waited by her side until she passed away. He later went on to be an extremely successful person, owing his own business and having a wonderful reputation.

When I met him in his mid-40s, despite all his wealth and success, deep sorrow poured out of him from every direction. He rarely smiled, and when he did you could see the pain in his eyes. For him life was not a place of fun feelings, but a place of doing. He had no context for his feelings – in fact, he had disassociated himself from any feelings at all from the moment his mom passed away. Thirty years later, he was still making himself suffer because he had made an unconscious agreement to not feel the beauty and joy of life. He chose suffering instead, because he felt responsible for his mother's pain.

I worked with him and shared ways for him to get in touch with his energy, and to come to the realization that he had issues about deserving love. We looked at the places in his life where he felt empty and I helped him re-language his life; to begin to create more of what he knew could be, rather than more of the past. He began to feel for the first time – just a little at first! But for a man who was not use to feeling anything, this was real progress. He was used to being numb and disassociated from his sacred sexual center, and he did not make love with feeling, and for sharing, but for the act of doing. In fact this area of our coaching challenged him the most and although he awakened considerably to his energy centers and was able to find joy in the little things in life, this was one area that he was tremendously blocked in. It simply required him to feel too much, and we all have our timing as to what's comfortable in our evolution. Most people don't like analyzing and watching their every move in times of transition, because it's quite fatiguing and it requires a great deal of resilience to look at all the areas of your life that you could improve upon.

If you've mastered one area of your life, particularly in business, where emotions are not valued, then dealing with the interpersonal can be very arduous and painful, or it can be invigorating and rewarding – it's up to you to decide how you will experience yourself. Once you begin to embrace the discomfort and allow for the humility and humanity behind your discoveries, the pain can be released, and you could move into a better feeling place, rather than hanging on to the suffering by ignoring it or denying it. The way out is the way in! In order to purge the pain you have to see what's causing the pain, but we often shut down certain centers in order to survive, and for many, surviving is more comfortable than thriving. People who are often afraid to feel their feelings are people who stay very top heavy, in their heads. I see them as a walking head with a detached body; they're not connected in to the lower regions of their body for fear of being overwhelmed, so they stay comfortably in the places they know they can achieve their best.

When you learn to align all your centers, the inevitability of a more loving reality is usually what ensues. Allowing the brain and mind time to interpret and analyze and then integrate with the heart is how you can become capable of fully melding the body, mind and soul. But first things first! If you don't know what it's like to be in your body then you have to have the experience of what that feels like, and in order to create this awareness you may need to stand in the presence of someone who can hold you in a loving light while you look at what's going on inside. It's like a light switch – there's always a current of energy running through the light, but until you switch it on it cannot shine. So we want to turn on the light that dwells within each of us to illuminate those areas of life that have been hiding in the dark. The light will only bring attention to what is already there. You can continue to sit in the dark and pretend that you're not surrounded by your thoughts, ideas, judgments and past occurrences, but the reality is that nothing leaves us! We are the best computer alive – we record and store it all consciously or unconsciously, it's all there inside us. When we give ourselves permission to see it, we can do so without the fear that we may accidentally bump into something dark and awful – we can pick and choose what we'd like to address next on our path to self-love and discovery.

When you run into a block, do not judge it or condemn yourself for being unwilling to overcome it – you just may have to address this one later. The important thing is that you have awareness that there is energy around this situation and ultimately, like the elephant in the room, it's going to have to be dealt with.

Although my businessman client was not able to address his sexuality at the time, he was willing to address other areas in his life. I left him with tools to encourage his ever-expanding awareness. He returned to me one year later to address the deeper layers and was presented with finding the real value of life which no longer based itself on a picture perfect life of material gain but on the bigger picture which was peace of mind and fulfillment from within. The sexual issues he encountered came to ahead when his marriage dissolved, which catapulted him into the opportunity to deeply love himself and to encounter new people from a more rooted connected core that was more authentic and present.

Now he may come back to this issue if it causes further discomfort later, and he will hopefully come to the other issues in due course.

Sometimes what we think others need may not actually be part of their life's mission, so we must make allowances for every individual's unique journey, and continually encourage their growth in whatever it is they are willing to do, and focus on the successes. Ultimately if the subject is pressing enough or the pattern is big enough it will be addressed sooner or later. So not to worry if you think that someone ought to be further along, they're right on course! Their speed is ever increasing; it just may not be at your pace. Have compassion for people's limitations; there are many factors to a multidimensional reality.

Allow, accept, accentuate as you surrender and remember.

One must accept what is, allow what will be, surrender to what has been and continually remember what life can be and embrace what we see. Life has many shades of grey and this is the beauty of the world. In order to move forward, we must follow certain guidelines to simplify the rhyme and reason to why it all is the way it is. Whatever way you choose is never the wrong way, it's just a way that will direct you toward your life's purpose. We are affecting each other at so many levels, and not everything resonates with all; life becomes super magical when we realize that whatever the search, whatever the church, whatever the country, there are always choices as to how you will live this existence.

I know the common denominator for all is to feel that our existence matters and to enjoy our lives. I believe that spirit is active in all things and that there are variations to the vibrations in which one chooses to live. We are not addicts because we love to suffer; we are addicts because we are afraid to suffer. We do not war because we believe we are wrong, we war because we are standing up for what we believe is right. In order to have life work for us rather than enslave us, we have to understand the path of least resistance and open ourselves to infinite possibilities. How can we all be right and how can so many be wrong? I can't imagine in a world of this size that there's only one way to enjoy existence. We are warring because we want to be right; well, I don't want to be right, I want to love! In order to be right you have to draw a line of separation and it's this division that creates the pain among nations. So in order to live a life of love rather than a life defending being right, and the cost that comes with that, we have to accept the differences.

We have to understand that at the end of the day, when we stop personalizing those offensive comments and look deep inside to see the real meaning behind hurtful words that may have been poorly articulated – is that every person shares, because every person is looking for understanding, to be known, to be accepted. We defend our position from self-preservation. In order to accept life and its circumstances we must make allowances for people and their freedom to express. Surrendering is the act of allowing; it's meeting people in love as opposed to fighting for the right to claim pain. Remembering is the act of acknowledging that you were born as, and reclaiming your birthright to a healthy, happy life, and the same for everyone else. No two people are alike, but we are all equal in the eyes of god. We are all on our mission. No one can direct you better than your own inspiration. Thank goodness we all have varying tastes or this world would be monochromatic; life would lose its flavor if we all didn't belong to different cultural values and preferences. Accept, allow, remember, surrender and most importantly embrace. When you can embrace what is, you can achieve freedom and detachment from the need to have anything, and you get into the habit of participating with everything. There are so many choices, so remember what is right for another may not be right for you. The judgment we place on others is the judgment we place on ourselves. To live in love you must surrender your need to be right and recognize the vastness of every individual's free will and personal choice.

Change: Does it really happen?

Why should you have to change? Change is a choice and it only happens when people are determined to make shifts in their lives and get out of their comfort zone. People choose not to change and adhere to their old structure because it provides safety, and we all want a stable life. Change is all around us, and how well you adapt to your changing environment can vary from moment to moment. Life is happening with or without your conscious contribution and the only way the world will improve is by individuals taking it upon themselves to look within.

Discover humanity within yourself and then reach out to the world around you. Change will only occur when you take personal responsibility for your contribution. You may not be a Bill Gates, leveraging billions of dollars, but you still have the free will to be the authority of how you think and feel as a contribution to the greater whole. If all you ever did was improve the way you are thinking, then you've done enough. As Gandhi said, be the change you want to see in the world.

Perhaps the change is not change at all, but a shift in perception, and this is the change that pivots you in the direction you have been seeking.

Defending your honor

Are you sure you want to defend your honor? What does it get you really? Ah, for the ego it says: I am valid, I am right, I knew the best way and I have proved my point. In life sometimes we have to take the offensive and sometimes we take the defensive. Sport is a beautiful demonstration of the polarities of life; you're either charging or being charged, but in either position you have to be alert because the game is on the line and every move you make creates the next action.

But how does standing up for yourself get you what you want? I spent my entire life defending my ego. I would fight in order to be heard, valued and validated, and I nearly killed myself in the process. Living a life of defense, being guarded and walking around being angry, victimized and blaming others, became a costly affair. I was always searching for my authentic self; I always desired to be free and easy, but with the heaviness of a victimized life and a sick body. I was in survival and if you threatened my survival with ideas that elicited change or humility or insinuated that I was a messed up person, I would attack. It didn't matter who you were, I did not like admitting that I was messed up and didn't know how to fix it.

So I chose to defend, attack and protect, I was very militant. But standing up for my life left me a lot of pain, isolation and separation. The depth of my loneliness and the depth of my inadequacy measured out the same. I was always seeking to fill the void with someone new, a new location or an object to satisfy my immediate needs, but the subtext was blurring over any experience I could achieve. That subtext was: I am unlovable, love hurt and I will prove it even if life seems to be going my way. I will prove my father right, that no one will ever put up with me because I am a pain in the ass. Great subtext to play under every interaction! This created a lot of failed relationships, because I expected every relationship to fail. I expected people would leave me – this was my story.

But somewhere deep inside was a girl who was just wanting love and had no idea how to get it. The only way I knew to give it was to be physical – so I spent my early 20's being promiscuous, always in search of a love that would last, that maybe this new person wouldn't discover that I was hurt and wounded. I never understood why so many loved me along the way; I was loved by many and when one left, another came to fill their place. The irony is that I made friends easily, everywhere I turned, because I was eager and had a good heart; at the core I was an honest person and people saw through my pain and saw into my being. But I never understood until later in life what it meant to see someone's potential, to see the actual person behind the façade of pain. I thought people must be able to see that I'm not loveable, and it would only be a matter of time before I pushed them away because I'm too demanding or controlling, because I found safety in these behaviors. My authentic self was somewhere to be discovered under the façade and remarkably, people always saw through the veil of pain and continued encouraging me along my path into self-love and awareness. It has been a 35-year endeavor and a 10-year conscious quest. What makes this possible is my commitment to address what arises daily with awareness and love.

Defense is such a futile activity, because the ego will never defend you back! It will always leave you in pain, because the cause you are standing up for is pride, and the need to be acknowledged for your efforts. But no one can acknowledge your efforts except you. You are the one you are fighting for; you are the one you want to acknowledge how amazing you are and how much you try to do your best. You are the one who has to validate you. When you win the fight and your ego has been vindicated, what do you win? But more importantly, what did you lose when you stood up for your cause? Did you let a relationship go? Did you sacrifice your integrity? Did you do or say something to elicit hurt in someone in the process of feeling better about yourself?

Did you hurt yourself? When you got what you wanted, did you then realize that after all the pain suffering and agony, it wasn't really worth it in the end?

CHAPTER TWO SUMMARY:
NO MISTAKES

1. Only by mis-taking life for what you thought was the right outcome do you learn how to adjust to what suits all concerned. This is where you extract deeper insights into what has occurred. From this place of seeing with awareness, what would you have done differently? Utilize this as a marker for the future.

2. Forgive yourself and others and embrace the wisdom of every situation as it rises, and see it as an opportunity to become a more whole person. The act of forgiveness is to free you from the pain you create from desiring others to be different from who they are. Do you want to be loving or do you want to be right? Compassion will allow you to humble yourself to see it from their perspective. It's not your responsibility to fix or adjust another's experience. All you ever experience is yourself, and all interactions lend an opportunity for deeper awareness in improving communication and neutralizing these emotional responses.

3. The exercise: For one week daily conjure all the people, places and situations that you perceive have created harm in your life and left you feeling hurt or resentful. Put them into your heart. Then imagine a large washing machine in

your heart; place one person at a time inside, then add your genuine forgiveness to the mix. Holding onto the pain is only hurting you and in order to move forward and receive a new outcome you have to let go of the past and start anew. Wash these individuals around in your heart; find the common denominator between you and them – find their divinity, forgive their humanity, step into their shoes for a minute and have compassion for their inability to be what you needed them to be.

One by one, release them down a grounding cord of light, which acts as a funnel into the earth, and allow the earth to absorb all the past hurts and pains and expectations or embarrassment.

Remember, most of the time the person you really need to forgive is yourself for having been enrolled in these painful interactions.

4. Create don't dictate. Life is to be felt and created from moment to moment, so when you're demanding or dictating how things ought to be, you may be missing out on an authentic life, and you may overlook the beauty of what that can bring.

5. Lighten up, have fun in your life, and let go. Once you begin to embrace the discomfort and allow for the humility and humanity behind your discoveries, the pain can be released, and you could move into a better feeling place, rather than hanging on to the suffering by ignoring it or denying it. The way out is the way in! It's like a light switch – there's always a current of energy running through the light, but until you switch it on it cannot shine. So turn on the light inside to give you the opportunity to illuminate

those areas of your life that have been hiding in the dark. We are the best computer alive – we record and store everything, consciously or unconsciously, it's all there inside us.

6. Allow, accept, accentuate as you surrender and remember. One must accept what is, allow what will be, surrender to what has been and continually remember what life can be and embrace what we see. We are not addicts because we love to suffer; we are addicts because we are afraid to suffer. In order to be right you have to draw a line of separation and it's this division that creates the pain among nations.

7. We have to accept the differences. Surrendering is the act of allowing; it's meeting people in love as opposed to fighting for the right to claim pain. Remembering is the act of acknowledging that you were born as, and reclaiming your birth right to a healthy, happy life, and the same for everyone else. When you can embrace what is, you can achieve freedom and detachment from the need to have anything, and you get into the habit of participating with everything.

8. Change is all around us, and how well you adapt to your changing environment can vary from moment to moment. Life is happening with or without your conscious contribution and the only way the world will improve is by every individual taking it upon him or herself to look within. Change will only occur when you take personal responsibility for your contribution. If all you ever did was improve the way you are thinking, then you've done enough.

9. Defending your honor: Defense is such a futile activity, because the ego will never defend you back!

3

PERCEPTIONS ARE EVERYTHING

When we create something, we always create it first in a thought form. If we are basically positive in attitude, expecting and envisioning pleasure, satisfaction and happiness, we will attract and create people, situations, and events which conform to our positive expectations.
~*Shakti Gawain*

"In 'Ali Baba and the Forty Thieves," Ali Baba faces the mountain and cries "OPEN SESAME." and the rocks slide apart. It is very inspiring, for it gives you the realization of how YOUR own rocks and barriers, will part at the right word.
~*Florence Scovel Shinn*

Truth vs. the filter and personal interpretation

Everything we experience and perceive comes through our own personal interpretation. This is why when someone is being examined in a court of law, they say: "In your own words describe to me what you experienced." What happens to us and what we see and do are completely subjective. This makes life tricky because we're always assuming we understand why people do what they do. We assume they need to do it like we do it, and if they're not seeing it from our point of view, then they are wrong. The only truth that exists is the universal truth, which is – all you experience is yourself. Therefore how can anyone ever speak on behalf of you or what it is you're experiencing? Life is phenomenal in this way because this is what creates the uniqueness and individuality of all in the matrix.

The truth of the matter is that there is only your truth, what you believe to be true. Yes, we have a shred understanding of words and concepts: we can all see that the car is yellow, but some may describe it as light yellow or canary yellow or bright yellow and so on. But if you have never experienced the color yellow, then yellow won't matter! You see truth occurs within the confines of education, experience and the ability to articulate through our limited language. This is why energy is so important; if we are unable to articulate what we're seeing we can still articulate what we're feeling. But if this is impossible, then there has to be a way in which we can communicate our truth, and that is through our body. The body never lies; it is the most authentic tool for communicating one's truth.

In order to know your own truth, you must be able to identify the filters through which you perceive life. Once you can clearly define the filters you speak through, you can then start to identify what is yours, what was taught to you, and what was socially ingrained in you in order to keep you suppressed.

The authentic self will never lie to you if you are willing to let go of the fancy things you dress it up as, and get real with what is being asked of you. If you're willing to pierce the veil of illusion you will find the answers awaiting your call.

Why are perceptions everything?

What you perceive you will believe. This is of course the only correct way anyone can conclude what is right for them. We understand ourselves through what we observe in our surroundings. Perception is self-interpretative, as this is the layer that will create separation between you and another. How can we ever dispute another's perception of life? But we do it all the time!

We undermine, negate and outright tell people that their perceptions are false. The funny thing is that once you discover the looking glass you peer through, you may begin to see that other people's perceptions are just that – their perceptions, and nothing to be feared. Perception is the filter through which we view the world; it's a gateway that distinguishes every individual and therefore creates responses, taste, choices and desires.

Your perception is ever changing, and as you continue to grow and strip away the pain, your perceptions of your experience change. When I look back on my life, I used to feel like I was a victimized, clumsy, angry soul and I felt a lack of purpose and lack of direction; my perceptions were based on my immediate experience at the time and on my immediate need to fulfill a momentary goal. As I have grown into a person who peers through the light of god, my perceptions of what I once experienced have changed. I now perceive life in a whole new light. I understand personal accountability in how I co-create everything I experienced, from my need to satiate my immediate goals, to constantly being affirmed for my physical attributes and bodily abilities. At the time I was not able to perceive that what I really wanted was to be loved for the essence of my being; all I knew was that I had to earn love by doing and being an aspect of who I am, not an embodiment of all that I am. So you see, perceptions change as we change, and what we once perceived as an injustice was really the thing that needed to occur in order for us to change.

Eating an apple? This apple is not you

This is an apple I am eating, but I am not the apple. "Apple" is the value and the meaning that we give it.

Life is all about experience, not ownership or entitlement; it is about the pure joy of experience. So I want to illustrate an example that will demonstrate why we are not what we eat, nor are we our emotions. We are the vessel in which these energies move throughout us, transient and always moving. I am not anger – I have anger, I experience anger, but I don't own anger. So ask yourself this: if I gave you an apple and you chewed, assimilated and eliminated this apple, is it your apple? Many of you may say: "Yes, you gave it to me, I ate it, it's mine." Or you may rethink this and say: "Well, yes you gave it to me, however it passed through me so no, it is not my apple, I never owned it, it was just an experience I was having."

Then if I asked you: is eating an apple good or bad? You might say 'good' because it's healthy for you; but if you're allergic to apples, then the experience won't be a good one. But the truth is – it is neither good nor bad, it just is. The value placed on the apple is nothing until you define it as good or bad, for you. The apple is neutral and, like life, is neither good nor bad, it just is. I am just experiencing it all as I go; I own nothing. I may have a home or a car, but if you distil it to its basic form, a home or a car is just energy. It's something I get to enjoy temporarily while I'm here in this physical body. This is why I make an effort to attach to nothing; as we saw with Cyclone Katrina, all that you own and all that you identify yourself to be can be gone in an instant – and then what is left? Just you the human, and without all your stuff, who are you? Without the ownership of my sickness, my anger, my boyfriend – who am I? We claim it all to be ours, but really it's just an experience we're having or sharing; nothing is ours personally, it belongs to the all.

We are just fortunate enough to have the means of acquiring things, we are not the apple – but when you eat the apple, it does become a part of you. So in that way, all that you are and all that you experience becomes part of you, yet nothing is yours. This gives rise to the understanding that we are one; all interconnected; not one thing would exist without the effort of all forces working together cooperatively to create the bigger picture. Every little thing counts, and the converse is – that nothing matters!

Moving from judgment to observation

This is one of the most important points in this book. We are nothing without the ability to interpret what is before us, however this may come as judgments. Now judgment in its own nature is perfect; it's what we're doing with these judgments that can become hurtful and life changing. Judgment in its pure essence is the ability to clearly interpret what it is you're experiencing; however if the interpretation of what you're experiencing is subjective, then that judgment may be positive or negative. So the approach I have found to curing the mind of its interpretation of what is right or wrong is to stand by and witness as an observer. It's not up to me to know what's right for another, as we are all having our unique experiences. It's not up to me to be judge and jury; I leave that to the Creator. However, it is my job to stay in a supportive, happy and loving place so that I can influence people through my example of being neutral to life. Only in neutrality can we encourage individuality.

Exercise:

Watch yourself for one week and see if you can just observe the happenings around you without making a judgment call on whether it's good or bad, right or wrong. Just experience yourself wanting to love and celebrate people in their choices, because their choice need not affect you. Choose the path of least resistance and say yes to what people are expressing. Notice what you experience then. This is one way to walk your talk in love.

A mother hits her child in public; the child begins to cry, then the mother drags the child away kicking and screaming. Your first knee-jerk reaction might be to condemn the mother and decide that the incident had spoiled your enjoyment of the day. The mind automatically judges, and then personalizes what happens. That's fierce judgment! What if you decided to observe and just witness how it made you feel, and you lifted yourself from the burden of having to persecute a total stranger? What if you just allowed the experience and asked yourself, can I send love to that situation? This takes a big commitment, to walk the talk in love.

You could have compassion for the abuser and the one experiencing the abuse, and recognize that both participants have their fair share of growing to do. You might even be compassionate to yourself for experiencing discomfort, and honor what that invokes; the scene may have triggered a response from your childhood. You may even be willing to say: "I don't know why they both attracted it, but I will lovingly allow people to learn in their own timing a more honoring patient way to communicate to each other."

You may even ask yourself: what would I do in this situation? And you may find that you would handle it differently according to how you were raised and taught. We can always put ourselves in another's shoes even if we're not a parent yet. We could also acknowledge the role that karma plays in every situation (if you believe in karma); maybe you subscribe to past lives where that particular mother and child are balancing some transgressions of the past. Or maybe we could get really present to energy – perhaps the mother and child were not energetically aligned, maybe they were out of their body and some other force had taken control…there are many scenarios we can create but the most important factor is: how do you experience it and handle the effect it has upon you? In most cases people can't help themselves – they jump to conclusions and begin defining someone's character. This is the fundamental problem of our world: we think we know how people ought to act.

Well, I guarantee that when someone is in love, they do not act this way, so what must we do to start walking our talk in love in every area of our life, moment to moment? We must begin to witness, and refrain from judging another person's process. We must allow people to grow at their own pace by lovingly encouraging them to be their best self. We must have compassion for the pain we all feel inside and we must not expect others to do it the way we would.

If we wanted to be an active observer in that situation we might have smiled at the mother to let her know that she wasn't alone, and that everyone gets frustrated. Maybe that smile of reassurance could have allowed her to soften and become present to her actions. Or you could have showered her with love and compassion, instead of passing her off to be an ongoing abuser destined to do it again. When we witness another, we are witnessing ourselves – so it pays to be as open and loving as possible.

Are you aligned in your thought, word, action and deed?

Witnessing another in their time of need and pain may not always align for you, as you too may be suffering. In order to align our thoughts, actions and words, we must cultivate a practice of self-dialogue, awareness and stillness, and incorporate this into our daily lives.

Do you do what you say? Integrity is about walking your talk…

Are you a person who follows through when you give your word? I often find that the reason people go back on their word is because they are 'people pleasers' and have a challenging time saying no. Instead of speaking their truth, they often agree to everything and then follow through with very little of what they say. Others are authentic in the moment when the promise is made, but then life happens and they overextend themselves and feel obligated rather than honored to participate. They don't have the courage to cancel and say they had a change of heart.

This is so common that we often don't recognize people when they are their word! Everyone has changed their mind at some time, and gone back on their promise. The problem occurs when people are counting on you to do and be what you present yourself to be. Disappointment ensues, followed by a lack of trust and sense of danger around planting any roots to grow your relationships forward.

In order to be a person of your word you must develop impeccable communication skills that will always prompt you to communicate your truth regardless of whether someone will be pleased or not. It is more painful experiencing the disappointment of something not happening, than the truth of what a person sincerely intends to do and is really capable of. We say yes to so much because on the one hand, we want to please ourselves but we also do it to receive the love and approval of another. Can you have the integrity to 'fess up and speak your truth without fear of hurting someone's feelings; can you risk the possibility that someone may not like you anymore once you speak your truth? If someone can't appreciate being told the truth they are yet to adopt the philosophy that nothing is ever personal. You have to know what you are willing to do in order to be a person of integrity.

When you can no longer be your word

I find that I often say yes, and then later I just don't have the energy to do it, so instead of leading someone on or feeling obligated, I communicate where I'm really at, rather than go somewhere or do something I don't really want to do. Whenever I have done this, when I have followed my intuition and just honored my needs, my friends may have gotten upset in the moment, but those who are truly my friends have understood. It's not personal. It is so much nicer for all involved when everyone participates with enthusiasm rather than a sense of obligation or fear that the opportunity will not present itself again. I find we often do things in fear because we don't want to be left out, so we go have the experience and realize that showing up with the agenda of not being left out makes you feel left out, even though you decided to participate! The reason behind why we do what we do tends to contaminate the experience.

Sometimes we attach ourselves to the idea of what it will be like, and then spirit will clearly give you signs and send you intuitions, giving you the choice to follow through or not. Sometimes all the anticipation and expectation of getting something leaves you feeling more disappointed than if you just allowed yourself to be in the surprise of it all. I've often gone to places because I've convinced myself that the only way to meet a person to be with is to make yourself available; so I force myself to go out in hopes of this chance encounter, as opposed to going out to have fun and see what I see! So often I will be disappointed because I won't find what I'm looking for. The key is to align yourself with what it is you're wanting to receive and then let the magic of sprit devise intelligent ways to bring it to you in any way sprit chooses! It doesn't always happen the way we think it should. Spirit is infinite in its ways to provide avenues of love, abundance and joy.

If you do something because you feel obliged to please another, more than likely you'll renege on your word, or show up late, or lack the appreciation for your experience.

Are you timely?

Do you have consideration for others and their time? It's important to honor the flow of your time and understand other people's timing as well. They say successful people are never late because they value the time of others. True or false? Who's to say that a person who is late doesn't value the time of others – perhaps they're just in their own timing and it can't be measured to the minute. I find that when I'm running 'late' it's often because I flow with my experiences and certain things have to occur within that time frame. So I either forgo the experience all together, or I show up 'late' when I am truly capable of giving my full participation. I find that if I am not fully caring for myself before I arrive somewhere, I may as well not show, because it will be a miserable affair, one that does not fit in with the flow of being open and fun.

In order to create a more timely life where people honor your time, you must honor your time first and foremost. I have a tendency to over-give and go beyond my time with my clients, because I love witnessing the unfoldment of the flow. Sometimes what I think needs two hours may only require one, or something that needs two may take eight days. Life is a guestimation of what we can accomplish given the circumstances and the intended goal, so we must be flexible with others and ourselves and plan enough space for incidentals. I love to be on time – that becomes a flow too – but we need to find compassion and allowance for those who do not operate within the normal standards of time, as it is better to celebrate the arrival of someone rather than punish them for arriving late! At least they arrived, which in itself says they care. People can become very vindictive when it comes to time and punctuality, and it is often the cause of many arguments. We take our precious energy and punish others rather than celebrating coming together. My experience of time is that when I am flexible and allowing, trusting that what needs to occur will happen, people always show just in time. They may not be punctual, but they're always in the right time for whatever the sharing is. And when I've put parameters on time, I'll usually set myself up to be late! When this happens, I allow a five-minute 'cushion' of time, I communicate who I am and I accept this about myself. Because I accept this, I find that I am non-resistant and the irony is that I now find myself to be more punctual than ever before!

People can lay huge guilt trips on you when they bust their ass to be on time and then you're late – really they're just angry at themselves that they rushed and didn't honor their needs to come when it felt right and not because they agreed to a particular time. Allocate yourself time for surprises – sometimes we get a call that is important, or an emotion arises; there are so many things that can prevent us from doing it right. Just know that when you choose to honor this in yourself, taking care of your own needs, others can honor it in you. So next time you're worried about being late, redirect your focus to being right on time and it will all unfold with more ease.

Claim what you choose…focus on what you desire, want and crave

Gratitude is the attitude! The number one thing I've found in common throughout the years with my clients is a lack of gratitude for the skills, relationships and material goods they already possess. I hear so often about the lack that permeates every area of their life. When it comes to appreciating our lives and demonstrating our gratitude, we just don't do it. We lack the simple knowhow, and worse, we aren't even aware that we are taking life for granted, because we've stepped into a role of entitlement and we expect so much. Happiness will never come from all your attainments and worldly possessions – happiness is a feeling; a way of being that can only be attained when you are reminded of what really counts in life. What really matters? Some may say the only thing that matters is your relationship to god or spirit, and for others what matters is your human relationships; others believe that financial gain is the reward to life and nothing else matters. At the heart of it all, God is in every relationship and material gain we possess and interact with. So appreciate and enjoy your personal relationship with the Creator and enjoy your honored relationships with others. Saying thank you and meaning thank you are two different things. Many people just roll those words off their tongue and don't even think about the meaning behind it. They just know where to place the words but the words lack passion and meaning, and are empty.

When we examine what's important to us, we can start to acknowledge that we spend a good majority of our lives in the pursuit of attaining something that makes us feel fulfilled, rather than appreciating what we already have. If life is what you make it, what are you making of your life? Is life one constant complaint of how you never have what you want or deserve? Are you always dissatisfied with what does appear before you? Do you perpetuate this attitude because your focus is always centrally themed around the not having and so you get more of the not having, more material for your drama to make it a juicier script? Do the lack, chaos and drama always find you? Are you expecting the worst? This is an easy dis-ease to remedy!

Find the ease in saying thank you and wake up to the reality of what is before you! When I was in India I would drive down dirt roads and stumble upon children laughing and playing in ragged clothes; they had the ability to turn a simple stick into a creative opportunity and they were gleaming with radiance for the simplicity of the life they led. They had barely enough food, they were sleeping outdoors, but their lives were beautiful (in my opinion, according to my perception of the scene). In fact the peace they possessed made them wealthier than most. They knew that there was more to the world than possessions – or they didn't know there was more, so they didn't lack for more. They had each other; they had the beauty of nature to fill their hearts. They appreciated life.

I gave some fruit to a young brother and sister – it wasn't even important what I shared with them, they were just so happy to be interacting with me; their smiles just filled my entire being from head to toe. I was beside myself with love and adoration for the humility, peace and ease I witnessed in these eyes of god. We did not speak the same language but the communication was clear – I was here to love and so were they. I didn't give them a gift – they gave me one, with the clarity to see that all we need is to give and receive in love and say yes to experiences that will remind us of who we are. The universal language of love always prevails.

The 'attitude of gratitude' is used so casually these days but I suggest you try it on for size and see how well it fits. Is it like an old hat, or is it something you need to break in, like a new pair of shoes? Are you in lack and longing for what you want or are you in continual appreciation of what you will have and what you already possess? Time will determine what is true for you and you may discover that if you don't stop to smell the roses in life; if you're too busy worrying about what's next that you neglect the moment at hand; if you aren't even present to the potential gift you are experiencing in this moment; then you miss the true gift of the ability to be present to perceive, receive and achieve all things. Love is all around you, let it in, thank your universe that people awaken to their true selves daily and can celebrate and share the love and adoration for the gifts you bear in participating in presence.

In America, Thanksgiving is such an opportune time to come together and share from the heart, to set old scores aside and acknowledge the energy and effort it takes to participate and play the game of life. This is a time to be very conscious of your thankfulness and to continue bringing in more awareness of how you can use this day as a marker and assessment of where you're. Perhaps you'll decide to make every day Thanksgiving, giving of your appreciation for all the things that come to you daily. Look around – there's no time to spare! What can you do in this instant to be more grateful for what you already have keeping in mind what you would like to have more of? I opt for love.

Exercise for gratitude (great-fullness):
- ☐ 5 Breaths Into Heart - When You Wake
- ☐ 5 Things You Love About Yourself - When You Wake
- ☐ 5 Things You Are Grateful For - When You Wake

Fake it till you make it.

We've all heard the expression, 'fake it till you make it' and I agree that sometimes, in the transition to receiving what is coming, you must feel as if it already is, and speak it to the universe that you accept what you have in gratitude. I'm not advocating that you go out and tell people a bunch of falsehoods; but I do recommend that you use your imagination to envision the reality of what you see for yourself. Make believe it is, until it can materialize in the physical form. My dear girlfriend always says, "I accept" when she encounters scenes of the life she is choosing to have today. "I accept this amazing relationship being demonstrated for me; I accept an abundance of love and support being presented to me in this moment; I accept that I am loved by the acts of love that are all around me; I accept life's blessings and magic forming around me."

CHAPTER THREE SUMMARY
PERCEPTIONS ARE EVERYTHING

1. Truth vs. the filter and personal interpretation: All you experience is yourself! Truth occurs within the confines of education, experience and the ability to articulate through limited language. If you're willing to pierce the veil of illusion you will find the answers awaiting your call. What you perceive you will believe. Perceptions change as we change, and what we once perceived as an injustice was really the thing that needed to occur in order for us to change.

2. Eating an apple? This apple is not you. It is neither good nor bad, it just is. Every little thing counts, and the converse is – that nothing matters!

3. Judgment in its pure essence is the ability to clearly interpret what it is you're experiencing; however if the interpretation of what you're experiencing is subjective, then that judgment may be positive or negative. Stand by and witness everything as an observer.

   Exercise: Watch yourself for one week and see if you can just observe the happenings around you without making a judgment call on whether it's good or bad, right or wrong.

4. Are you aligned in your thought, word, action and deed? In order to do this, you must cultivate a practice of self-

dialogue, awareness and stillness and incorporate this into your daily life.

5. Do you do what you say! Integrity is about walking your talk.

   In order to be a person of your word you must develop impeccable communication skills that will always prompt you to communicate your truth regardless of whether someone will be pleased or not.

6. When you can no longer be your word. If you do something because you feel obliged to please another, more than likely you'll renege on your word, or show up late, or lack the appreciation for your experience.

7. Are you timely? Next time you're worried about being late, redirect your focus to being right on time and it will all unfold with more ease.

8. Claim what you choose. Focus on what you desire, want and crave.

9. Gratitude is the attitude!
   If life is what you make it, what are you making of your life? What can you do in this instant to be more grateful for what you already have keeping in mind what you would like to have more of? I opt for love.

   Fives – an exercise for gratitude (great-fullness):

*5 Breaths Into Heart- When You Wake

*5 Things You Love About Yourself- When You Wake

*5 Things You Are Grateful For- When You Wake

10. Fake it till you make it.

Make believe it is, until it can materialize in the physical form.

4

PRACTICAL TOOLS FOR THE LIFE YOU CRAVE

"I can tell you that anything that happens in the physical body will happen in the pattern of the energy fields first.

The body is a self-healing organism, so it's really about clearing things out of the way so the body can heal itself."
~*Barbara Brennan Quote*

"In truth, we always ask for definite leads just what to do; you will always receive one if you ask for it. Sometimes it comes as intuition, sometimes from the external."
~*Florence Scovel Shinn*

Checking your energy system: The way out is the way in.

In order to create the changes you desire, you must have a deep understanding of how the mechanism works. You are that mechanism! Every sage throughout history has discovered the same solutions for inner peace and fulfillment – take the journey inward, inside where all the answers lie. So the way out of pain and suffering is to go into the pain and suffering in order to perceive what is there. We are all comprised of the same matter and this matter is aptly defined as energy...we are energy. So, first things first, we are going to scan the energy field to have a better understanding of what we feel!

STEP 1: SCANNING

Visualize a scanner with a red laser light that crosses up and down over text, reading the information to be transferred into your computer. We're going to do the same with your body. Pretend your body is this piece of text, which you will scan from head to toe, receiving any communication you can about how it feels.

Does it feel empty and depleted?

Does it feel heavy and congested?

Does it feel attached or corded into anyone other than you?

We will go into more details in a minute, but for now just sit silently and see what is there.

Good. Now that you have scanned your body you may have more awareness about what's going on inside. If this is so for you, excellent work! If not, no problem. I'm here to teach you a quick and easy sequence that will provide you with the steps to self-awareness to achieve self-mastery.

STEP 2: GROUNDING CORD – USE IT LIKE A FUNNEL

Grounding is one of the most important things you can do before initiating any further action toward clearing your energy.

Imagine a golden column of light that is anchored at the base of your spine, at the sacrum; make it as wide as the circumference of your hips, and as deep as you can, so you may use it as a funnel later.

Imagine this column of light as a cord, dropping deep into the core of the earth until it hits the molten lava. Feel the connection between you and earth, a rooted feeling like you are deeply planted with roots, immovable with a solid foundation.

This cord will be a multi-functioning cord: it will ground your energy and it will also be used as a funnel to release unwanted clutter and congestion from the mind and Heart. Like a plumber we like to have a place to release all the s—t. This funnel can be used to flush out the past and to create space for present day awareness, free and clear. This is a simple and easy exercise: we can ground anywhere. This is especially important for those who like to lift out of their body from time to time. You can ground your energy into Mother Earth at any time – sitting, standing, walking, talking, driving – it can be done anywhere. There is no single conventional or traditional way to do this; what matters most is that you're aware of this procedure and then you can apply it anywhere when necessary. You can also imagine the roots of a tree coming out of your feet and dropping those deep into the layers of the earth's ground, this is also another easy tool for grounding your being.

STEP 3: THIRD EYE AND HEART CHAKRA: A QUICK CHECK FOR CONGESTION.

I've discovered that in order to feel joy and stay in love we must be able to feel ourselves as we truly are, without congestion and filters coating the path.

It's like a good snow storm – you know, once the snow melts, there's a whole other world going on down underneath but until you clear the way you'll only see the surface. The trick is to uncover the foundation of your being and then when it rains or storms you have the choice to either leave it as it is, or clear the way and feel the foundation. Either way is correct, however the more in tune you become with who you truly are, anything covering the way seems to be a heavy-weighted distraction and you become eager to understand what is there without judgment, just observation.

The two most important gateways for understanding your foundation, which is the seat of the soul, are the heart and the third eye (the 6th chakra, between the eyes). The third eye is where your perception of joy resides, where you can enjoy the moment without concern for the next, because you are clear and free to show up in the awesomeness of who you really are. The second position of great importance is the Heart (the 4th chakra); this is where it all begins and ends. The heart is the gateway to feeling the oneness, feeling god's grace and the faith that we're here in it together, but in order to access the Heart clearly and feel into all your experiences, you must have clear sight and have removed the filters and veils blocking your perceptions of the reality you are truly living in.

I suggest that you do this exercise in private so you can be comfortable expressing the physical self without being concerned about other people's judgments. However if you're comfortable in your being, then this can be done anywhere. The tools to be used on the physical body have been designed to make what you're doing more tangible and as a form of entrainment...after a while, you may not need physically bathe and sweep your field; you will be able to do it within your mind's eye. You will discover what works for you over time.

Gathering the energy to have a clear picture of what opportunities lie before you.

Exercise 1:

You can do this seated or standing.

Imagine your energy field has a color or texture. You may interpret what you're experiencing or envision this to be black clouds or smog, especially if you're not feeling your best. (I'm not implying that your energy is murky and grey – but we can all have moments when we feel grey or sad, and this generates an image that you can grab onto.)

If this visual works for you, then imagine reaching high into the sky with both your hands, gathering the energy that is around you into a little black ball in front of your face. This will look like a swift sweeping and grabbing motion.

You can also reach into your third eye and pull or unscrew any energy that feels heavy or congested. Reach out to the sides, in front of you and above you, and little by little you will have formed a ball of energy in front of you. When you feel you have gathered all the energy there, close your eyes and ask yourself: "What am I not wanting to see, hear, feel or say in my life right now?" Or you may ask the ball of energy: "Is there a message here for me?" Sit quietly and wait to receive a message from your higher self. The reply will come; command it and know it and you will always be amazed at the willingness of the universe to supply you with the truth when seeking. Taking inventory daily reaps major rewards and swift results as you deepen into what is and that translates as deeper love and acceptance for yourself and the world around you.

Once you've identified what's in the ball of energy and what you need to do to acknowledge, remember, forgive or release, then imagine the ball lifting out of your hands. If you used the visual of the darkness, then as the ball lifts, you will watch the veil of darkness fall away, dissolving into the earth as the ball emerges in its true form of golden light energy. Watch as it rises into the sky and disperses into a billion particles of golden dust. Now you have begun to release the accumulated energies of the day.

Third eye clearing.

As mentioned before, the third eye is the seat of your joy. If this area is congested you will have misconceptions about how you view and perceive the world. So the next step is to go to this area and see how it feels. Do you feel foggy, hazy and congested? Or is it light and airy? Over time you will begin to know the difference, but it will take daily practice for you to slow down and tune in. The easiest way for me to perceive the energy within and around my headspace is to roll my eyes a little up and inward. It may look funny to an outsider as you expose a little of the whites of your eyes!

To do this, sit still for a moment, and then feel the energy around your third eye, from left to right, and spin or scan the energy around you. Then once again you will ask yourself: What am I not wanting to see or perceive, hear, feel or say in this moment? Or you can also ask yourself: what is appearing before me? What do I feel or hear now?

Wait for an answer, if one does not come immediately. In the meantime, in order to begin the sloughing-off process and clearing the way to seeing what's there, imagine a spinning disc cutting diagonally through your Third Eye area, reaching just a little further out to the sides of your head. Now imagine the color of this energy as indigo – or you can also keep it neutral and make it from variations of luminous light in the metallic range. Spin, spin, spin away, this will clear the heaviness of the day. You may even notice that eyes that once felt sleepy have a renewed lightness and brightness and you feel more alert. So you're spinning, and awaiting an answer. This is a twofold process; you are clearing and receiving insight at the same time. Once you understand what it is you are not wanting to see, sit with the information for as long as you need to process the next course of action. It could be forgiveness, moving to the heart, letting go, letting other people go, etc. Clarity will come, answers will appear and you will feel empowered by your ability to perceive the source of your pain. What's troubling you may not even be something hurtful – it could just be information that is needed in order for you to take right action. Once you've been guided to what it is you need to perceive, you will know if going into the heart to forgive is necessary.

Heart Chakra

Place both hands in the middle of your chest, overlapped not intertwined. Then place one hand over the other symmetrically and begin to feel the rise and fall of your heart.

Breathing

Close your eyes and begin to slowly breathe in through the nose and exhale with an open mouth, expelling the air. Feel your heart. Is it rising out of your chest? Does it feel tight? Are you even able to access your breath in this area? You may find this is an area that needs strengthening, but persist in your observation and experience of just sitting with your breath for a few minutes. Do you have a shallow breath? Do you feel relief when you breathe deeply, or is it hard for you to slow it down and get into your body? Discover who you are by tuning into your body and its natural tendencies.

I breathe extremely deeply when I encounter situations that feel uncomfortable; in order to cope and open to what is before me. Many people have a tendency to take swift little breaths and when asked to breathe deeply, find it challenging to pull into the heart area. Who are you and what is your level and ability? If you find that breathing is not an easy thing for you, there are people out there who can work to help you with isolated breathing. It is my opinion that once you've mastered the breath, then clearing becomes a piece of cake, because you're anchored in life-force, regenerating you to your restorative self. One practice I highly recommend is Network Spinal Analysis; they will teach you how to use your breath precisely to move energy and unblock pathways.

You can find a local practitioner in your area (in the U.S.). This in fact was the first work that unlocked my heart and opened up my capacity to breathe with awareness.

For those of you who would like a personal practice to unlock your breath I recommend massaging your chest daily. You can start at the clavicles using both your hands and move your way around until you come to the center of your breast bone, this tends to be very sensitive however stay with it and continue applying pressure. You'll find with the consistency of massaging your own heart center the sensitivity will subside and a deeper ability to breathe and connect to yourself will ensue. I generally do this when I am bathing – it's a perfect time to take a few moments for you. While you're there move your hands down to your feet and give them a few squeezes while you hit on a few pressure points, this will also open up the energy for groundedness and open heartedness. Remember to massage the toes too.

Look into reflexology if you'd like to understand the power of healing that occurs for each pressure point and how each one correlates to an organ in your body. But just remember its not about the knowing that makes the shift – it's the doing, so play around and explore yourself and feel into what feels good or releasing to you. The understanding of what it all means can come later. I also highly recommend a weekly yoga practice – this opens all the energy centers and focuses your breath as you move from posture to posture. Any style can benefit you. Some of my favorite yoga styles include Kundalini Yoga, which is deeply geared toward enhancing your spiritual practice through breath and sound. I also love hot yoga or Bikram yoga, however I prefer a fusion of Bikram and power yoga in a heated room. Many studios offer these fusion courses. Yoga is not only a physical practice but also a journey inward and a lifestyle of practicing a life of living in waking consciousness.

While you are in the heart, this is a good time to examine if there are any people, places or situations that call for your forgiveness. One way to empower our lives is to take all things into our heart; then it is no longer a threat outside of us, but something we can heartfully embrace. One by one, place these people/places/situations there and imagine cleansing yourself of the hurt, hatred resentment or pain from these interactions. Imagine a washing machine in your heart; you're going to wash away the pain, cleansing yourself and others, adding the soap of forgiveness and acceptance. You can now use your funnel to drain the murky water into the earth. I've found that the person who needed my forgiveness the most was me, for having involved myself in these situations to begin with! This technique was given to me by my chiropractor, Sai-Ling Michaels.

Lastly – and this really opens the energy field – give yourself a head and temple massage. You can do this when you shower; just make a concerted effort to focus more pressure and feel around the temples to release any tension that may be pent up bringing, your awareness there. If you start to massage your head daily you'll feel more open, connected and relaxed.

Exercise daily for a week: Sit quietly for a few moments each day for one week and conjure people, places and situations that need your forgiveness, things that are holding you in a painful place; resentments, injustices, judgments of people's behaviors.

Free yourself from the burden of having to know what is right for another or from feeling victimized. Empower yourself now by taking charge of how you're going to feel and how you will create different experiences by releasing lessons and experiences from your past. For example, I did this for my fifth grade teacher, who had humiliated me in front of my peers. I never forgot the feelings this elicited in me, so forgiveness was vital. By freeing myself of her and many others, I created room in my heart to breathe and receive the new.

Take one week and ask, forgive, wash and release the water to the earth, and then once you've reconciled with each person, you can then release them and the situation down your funnel grounding cord. You will feel like you just lightened your load! Now you can take all the energy that was invested in harboring ill-will towards others and create, with intention, a new course of action towards a life of empowered choice and deliberate action, centering all that you do in the heart in order to satisfy your desire to give and receive love.

OK: quick review!

- Sweep your energy field
- Ask yourself: what is my message?
- Release the ball of energy into the heavens
- Tune into the third eye
- Ask yourself: what am I not wanting to see right now?
- Determine if it is clear or congested – this will determine the amount of introspection necessary to clear this area
- Spin a disc of illuminated energy until the congestion is clear
- Step into the heart region and begin to breathe, placing both hands in the middle of your chest, overlapped not intertwined
- Place one hand over the other symmetrically and begin to feel the rise and fall of your heart
- Breathe slowly in through your nose and out through your mouth
- Massage heart and feet
- Use the washing machine of forgiveness and acceptance

- Drop people, places and situations down your grounding cord once you've reconciled these relationships
- Drain water down funnel
- Begin anew in an open and free heart.

Aura Awareness

The Aura is the light body that emanates a field of energy around the physical body. The aura has colors that correlate to various emotional states of being. For our purposes here I want to encourage tapping into the aura in order to feel the extension of the light body that exists around you. Close your eyes and tune into your body; extend your awareness out further and you'll be able to sense what's around you. This is also helpful when doing the third eye clearing as you are really tapping into the entirety of your being energetically, mentally, physically, emotionally, and etherically. See what you discover. Do you feel texture, sound, color, lightness, heaviness, do visions appear?

A great friend, Walker Whelan, an amazing conveyer of the light, gave me an exercise years ago that I found to be helpful in sweeping the energy field when I'm feeling heavy and I want to lighten up:

Exercise: Tornados of light and Golden Wash

Imagine light 20 feet in every direction around your body. Now imagine the power of washing your body and auric field with this light as it gently caresses the entirety of your being. Once you feel this beautiful cleansing you may now turn this light into a twisting tornado, coming from all directions, sweeping your field and picking up any remaining distortions and carrying them off into the heavens or down into the ground. Let this be fun; use your imagination to interpret how to spin and use your tornados of light to assist you in lightening your field.

Once you've experimented with all the various tools, you may use your imagination to conjure images and colors to create a field of energy that supports your new reality of waking consciousness, adopting love as the foundation of your being and allowing for infinite possibilities. Notice what appears! All the power you desire lives within your reach as you go inside and focus on the life of your choice. Let this become your new reality expanding in all directions, becoming your current reality. Remember the universe has no concept of time or space so create from here and now the reality you prefer to be in and let the universe coordinate that vision as your current reality. If you feel it as if it already is, you may witness drawing the circumstances that support how you are feeling.

Chakra spin

Visualizing the energy centers and strengthening your energy body by utilizing awareness around you.

Chakra is derived from the Sanskrit word for wheel or turning. Chakras, more accurately described as a vortex or a whirlpool, are the points found in the human body that relate to the major centers of the physical body. We work with the chakras to create harmony and cohesiveness to our energy field.

Most people use 7 chakras within the body field, but I use a 12-chakra system to clear my energy; I like to go into the higher dimensions of this third dimensional body. If you would like to learn more about the chakras, read 'Anatomy of the Sprit' by Carolyn Myss. She discusses the 7 chakras in depth.

My focus is to teach you how to best utilize your energy, even if you don't know the meaning of the chakras; whatever you do will begin the pathway to awakened awareness, and you can understand the inner workings and meanings of it all later.

I begin with spinning a disc of light in the 11th chakra first. Now this chakra can be any color you choose – in fact I encourage you to ask yourself, what is my color? And see what appears. I have assigned colors for the lower chakras, but the 11th and 12th I leave up to you. (You can however use your own intuition with respect to the 7-chakra color system because we are all unique, and what applies to one may not apply to all. So find you're unique take on it.)

The 11th chakra is way up high in the sky – you can determine that for yourself. I look up into my Third Eye to access my inner sight when going into these higher realms.

Begin to spin a disc of energy at the 11th chakra, feeling for clarity and ease of movement. We're going to go down the chakras in odd numbers, and up in even numbers: Down: 11, 9, 7, 5, 3, 1, then up to 2, 4, 6, 8, 10 and 12.

At 9, I like to spin gold, but once again, ask yourself what is the color for my highest good...and watch and see. I've found even without using color, just the action of spinning will elicit the effect. Know that intention is key to creating everything, so make this yours by customizing this L.O.V.E. Sequence according to your preferences.

Spend about 30 seconds to a minute in each chakra – the better you get at spinning your own energy, the less time it takes and the quicker you can perceive what may be out of alignment.

Suggested colors for the chakras:

12th chakra (above the body) = ask your own intuition

11th chakra (above the body) = ask your own intuition

10th chakra (above the body) = ask your own intuition

9th chakra (above the body) = ask your own intuition

8th chakra (above the body) = ask your own intuition

7th or crown chakra located at the top of your head = violet

6th or Third Eye chakra = indigo

5th or throat chakra = any shade of blue, use your imagination

4th or heart chakra = green

3rd or solar plexus chakra = canary yellow

2nd or sacral chakra = orange

1st or base chakra = primal red.

You can spin your chakras however you see fit; this is a very loose version of working with these energies, as you will discover what feels right to you over time. You may only enjoy working with the traditional 7 chakras, but in order to know what works, try experiencing it all. I was given this system by a healer named Nicholas and I modified it to work for me. I had been working with the chakras for years in a traditional way of going in one direction, but Nicholas encouraged going from top down with the odds and cycling back up with the evens. When I asked him why, he said 'It just works,' and I chuckled because that was my personal experience of it. It just feels right and it works. You will find what is best for you over time.

However I will say that running these energies daily will create awareness and integration of the energy-being more swiftly, and will tune you into what you are thinking and being, by bringing your attention to isolated areas of your being. I scan my chakras all the time and once you learn the meanings, you will find that pains correlate to emotions, organs and colors in each area. For example, throat infections may mean a fifth chakra disturbance stemming from the inability to speak one's truth to self or another; this could disrupt the connection between the heart chakra and the crown chakra disempowering your connection to a higher power. Even if you spin every chakra for 15 secs, that's better than nothing at all – you will still have cleared much, and the more awareness you apply to your space the better you will feel.

MAIN CHAKRA CENTERS

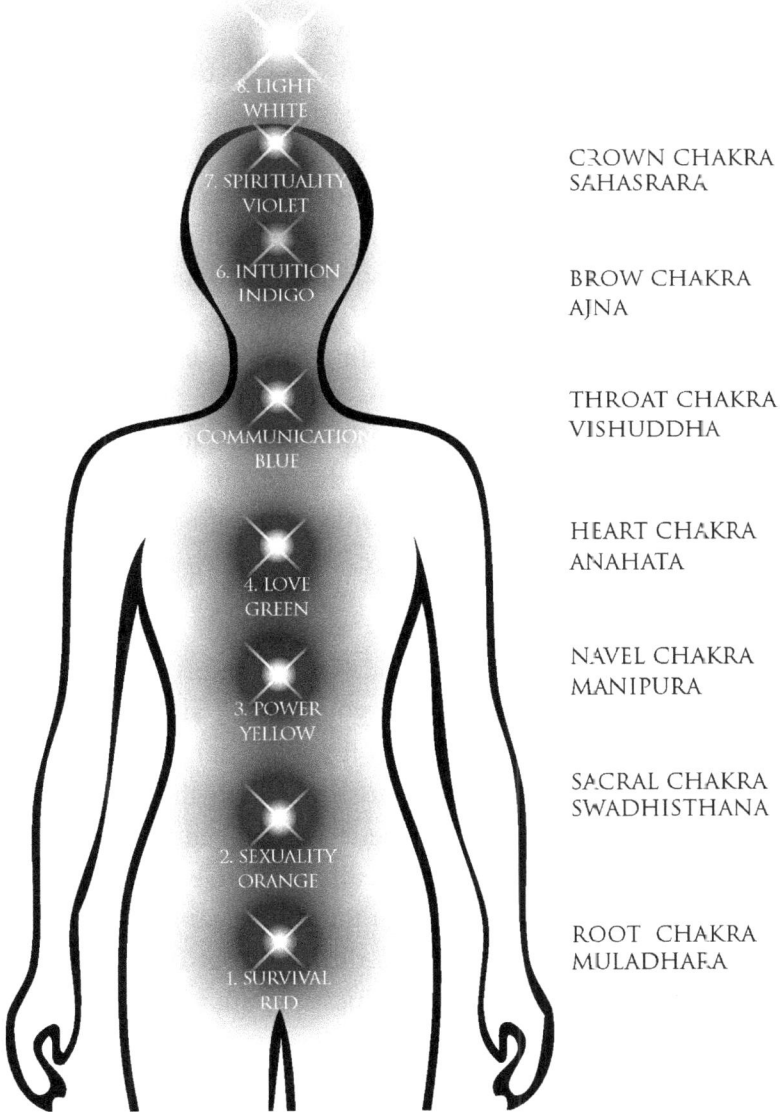

8. LIGHT
WHITE

7. SPIRITUALITY
VIOLET

6. INTUITION
INDIGO

5. COMMUNICATION
BLUE

4. LOVE
GREEN

3. POWER
YELLOW

2. SEXUALITY
ORANGE

1. SURVIVAL
RED

CROWN CHAKRA
SAHASRARA

BROW CHAKRA
AJNA

THROAT CHAKRA
VISHUDDHA

HEART CHAKRA
ANAHATA

NAVEL CHAKRA
MANIPURA

SACRAL CHAKRA
SWADHISTHANA

ROOT CHAKRA
MULADHARA

Calling in the angels for assistance.

Over the years I've discovered so many ways to connect with my higher self and I've come across so many healers who use many different modalities. However, the healers who are consciously working with the angels and invoking their presence are the ones with whom I've had the most profound healings. Some of you may think it's a bit corny to call on your angels for assistance – maybe it seems fictitious, or perhaps you'd like to believe we all have personal angels but you're not sure if it's possible. Well, I have always been a person who is willing to try new things – in fact the only way I've ever discovered the efficacy of anything is through my willingness to experience all the variations and seemingly offbeat passages to love and awareness. I have discovered that angels exist; in fact they love to assist us on our path. The Bible speaks of angels and throughout history you will see depictions of angels in some of the greatest masterpieces of our times.

So let's get right in and keep it super simple. When in need of healing assistance, a helping hand, Divine intervention, more fun and play, or something to restore your faith, I suggest you call on the angels. If you think this is a bit too far out – it never hurts to try! In the beginning I had a hard time with this too. In fact I thought that the angels worked better if invoked through someone else and I doubted my ability to really be connected to the angelic realm. We are all connected – but the angels cannot come to assist us if we don't call upon them, as they will not interfere with free will, but they will guide us to our highest path if we so choose and if we ask.

I make this statement before I do any healing work and I intermittently call upon them for guidance throughout the day; I also call upon them when I do the L.O.V.E sequence. I strongly believe that working with the angels amplifies the radiant body and can transmute people, places and situations more expeditiously. If you are not aware of which angel to work with, or you've never even thought of working with an angel, then here are a few names of the most powerful angel to begin with: Archangel Michael, Archangel Uriel, Archangel Gabriele, Archangel Raphael, Archangel Metatron. You can do more research on the Internet to find out what each angel's specialty is, that way you know who to call upon in various situations. But once again if you're not into researching, then calling on any or all of these angels will create an immediate connection for assistance. I also suggest you read Doreen Virtue's books on angels; or buy an angel deck of cards and have fun with the messages the angels deliver via this medium.

Affirmation Statement: I call upon my angels, guides and guardians to guide and lead me to my highest good in all areas of my life. Bring me people, places and situations that support the enfoldment of my life in a graceful, blissful and fulfilling way for the highest best. I am open to receive inspiration and signs as a verification of my communication with the Divine. I send the light ahead and I ask that the highest will be done. I let go and trust that whatever it is I am experiencing throughout the day has been Divinely orchestrated because I called upon my support team of angels. I know that sprit is always moving me toward my desired outcome. I find the joy in all that I experience even when it gets hard and I have resistance to my circumstances. I trust my guidance.

Heaven and earth are passages to release.

1. Release images into earth

Carrie is an amazing healer I worked once, many years ago. She taught me that the images I was feeling and seeing that may have been hindering my process could be released into the earth –

it was no longer necessary to carry them in my field. Simply release the images into mother earth and voila! Freedom ensues; they no longer have a hold on you.

You need to have your grounding cord connected at the circumference of your hips, making it a wide column of light to use as a funnel for releasing images from the heart and mind. You can also envision the column upward toward the heavens out through the crown of the head to be released to the heavens. Wherever you choose, it will be what is most appropriate for you – be flexible, be guided. There is no one right way to release, use your imagination perhaps you'll find a new rendition of this same concept and find it equally effective.

2. Washing Machine Heart forgiveness

As discussed before, the key to making this tool work is that in order for you to take back your power you invite everything into your heart space. Once it is in your heart it can no longer have control or power over you, as you are now embracing it in the most sacred part of you.

Visualize a washing machine in your heart or a waterfall. Place people or experiences into it in order to cleanse and renew. In the Jewish tradition, the women take a 'mikvah' (full immersion in water) in order to cleanse themselves for the purification of their body, mind and soul before they enter into sacred connection with their mate. This purification process is something we can all make more ceremonial for the renewal of our souls and our relationships. Like the fallen drops of the sky that kisses the earth we feel renewed once the last raindrop has fallen – there is freshness in the air.

So we place people, places and situations into our heart to regain our power and wash or cleanse these energies until we feel we have purified them into a state of neutrality where we can then release and drain the waters down the funnel (grounding cord) into the earth.

We can ask for for-giving for-caring for-sharing to occur with the person or thing at hand and identify what that situation made us feel. We can be compassionate to what occurred, seeing it from both sides, and we can ask to see the benefits of the experience in order for us to release the past and move forward with an empowered heart, knowing that all experiences serve to benefit us on our journey to bring us into alignment with our higher purpose.

3. Tornado of light and the golden wash

Again, as discussed earlier, this is also another effective tool for purifying the energy field. You can also use golden suns to quench the cells of your entire being. Imagine golden suns coming into the top or crown of your head. Let this beautiful warm light spread throughout your entire body, revitalizing every cell with energy. You can use as many suns as you like until you feel thoroughly quenched and drenched in light.

Carrie the healer also gave me this visualization years ago and I have found it to be an effective tool. I also like to imagine golden balls of light streaming in through the crown and vibrating every one of my cells into complete restoration, revitalization and renewal.

No matter who you are there is always something to discover within and around you; feelings are always there to be uncovered. In the inquiry you can discover so much about yourself and your surroundings. Just asking a question can promote a conversation. Simply ask the question: what more can I see today about who I am and who is around me? When we look outside we are still looking within and vice versa, as everything is an aspect of you.

As long as it is in your field of observation it becomes a relevant factor in your reality in order to make you more aware of the contrast life brings. It is up to you how you want to perceive and identify with your current reality. Remember this: you are only ever talking to yourself. If you feel alone remember when you tap into the all-one you know there is a greater force thrusting you forward to the right people, places, and situations.

All of these tools facilitate the refinement of your immaculate instrument in order for you to be a concentrated focuser, with conscientious intentions to have the life you crave today.

Awareness of self, body, mind, and soul will lead you into living a life of presence and an awakened heart, where you are capable of compassion for the contrast of living a life of duality and knowing your own unity.

THE L.O.V.E. SEQUENCE
L.IVING O.PENLY V.IBRANTLY E.NERGETICALLY

Ground your energy with a column of light out of your sacrum.

Gather energy into a ball, ask what is the message or communication, dialogue, send love, release to heaven or earth.

Golden wash 20 feet above your head, golden body wash for reclaiming energy invite people, places and situations into the heart, rinse, for-give, love and then release down your funnel of light into mother earth.

Cutting ties from people: golden wash, infinity sign release. Imagine an infinity sign – the figure of 8 – put your face in one side and the person you are cutting ties with in the other, split the infinity sign and release both faces into different directions.

Chakra cord cutting: facing one another, imagine a sharp object like a sword or machete and use it to cut the cords through the 7 physical chakras in the body, pat the energy that is returning to you into your body and return energy into their body. Do the same from behind then walk in opposite directions. Imagine uncorking or unscrewing a cord in an individual chakra – let it spiral back into that person…fill the hole with light where you release the connection.

Scan the body to see who is occupying your space or see if there are any vacancies. Always continue awareness of your grounding cord.

Aura awareness: imagine pulling in your aura from all sides to encapsulate your body. Depending on how you feel, this can range from 12 inches out all the way into your body. Seal yourself up in your own liquid golden light suit. It encapsulates the front, back, and sides of your being, depending upon what is comfortable to you. I prefer close into my body, some like it even 24 inches out. You can use a liquid golden body (light) suit or super hero suit, you can even give your super hero suit a name; feel your own emanation. For insulation of your energy field, feel your shine when you are contained within your own given parameters.

Third eye awareness: place hands (hands emanating light) on head front to back or side-by-side. See a curtain opening in your mind's eye onto a stage of pure white light. Spin a sphere or disc of light through your third eye center; ask if there is a message. Ask yourself what are you not wanting to see, feel, hear or say in this moment, become present through awareness by clearing the congestion.

Heart awareness: massage the heart. Take deep breaths in through the nose and out through the mouth. Feel what is there: fullness, depletion, sadness, frustration, release these into the earth through a column of light. Massage the reflexology points in your feet or just massage in general around the foot area, remember to massage the toes too. Massage the head and temples to release energy.

Your pictures, thoughts, emotions and worries can all ground into the earth through your grounding cord or can be transmuted into heaven. Imagine angels swooping in and carrying these energies upward as they dissolve back into a billion particles of light.

Clearing and opening chakras: odd numbers first, starting with the 11th chakra downwards, then 9,7,5,3,1, resuming upward with the 2nd chakra all the way to the 12th chakra. Imagine a sphere or disc of light like a Frisbee cutting through each chakra. Chakra colors – these can be your choice, they may vary and change for you, ask yourself: is this my color?

Imagine a tornado of light through your energy body, starting at the crown, then on each side of your aura, grounding the energy into the earth.

CHAPTER FOUR SUMMARY:

PRACTICAL TOOLS FOR THE LIFE YOU CRAVE

1. Check your energy system. The way out is the way in. You are that mechanism! So the way out of pain and suffering is to go into the pain and suffering in order to perceive what is there. We are energy.

STEP 1: SCANNING

Pretend your body is this piece of text, which you will scan from head to toe, receiving any communication you can about how it feels.

☐ Does it feel empty and depleted?

☐ Does it feel heavy and congested?

☐ Does it feel attached or corded into anyone other than you?

STEP 2: GROUNDING CORD – USE IT LIKE A FUNNEL

Imagine a golden column of light anchored at the base of your spine, at the sacrum, the circumference of your hips. Imagine this cord dropping deep into the core of the earth until it hits the molten lava. This cord will be a multi-functioning cord: it will ground your energy and it will also be used as a funnel to release unwanted clutter and congestion from the mind and heart.

STEP 3: THIRD EYE AND HEART CHAKRA: A QUICK CHECK FOR CONGESTION

The two most important gateways for understanding your foundation, which is the seat of the soul, is the heart (the 4th chakra) and the third eye (the 6th chakra, between the eyes).

When you feel you have gathered all the energy there, close your eyes and ask yourself: "What am I not wanting to see, hear, feel or say in my life right now?" Or you may ask the ball of energy: "Is there a message here for me?" Sit quietly and wait to receive a message from your higher self.

Once you've identified what's in the ball of energy and what you need to do to acknowledge, remember, forgive or release, then imagine the ball lifting out of your hands. If you used the visual of the darkness, then as the ball lifts, you will watch the veil of darkness fall away, dissolving into the earth as the ball emerges in its true form of golden light energy. Watch as it rises into the sky and disperses into a billion particles of golden dust. Now you have begun to release the accumulated energies of the day.

THIRD EYE CLEARING

If this area is congested you will have misconceptions about how you view and perceive the world. Do you feel foggy, hazy and congested? Or is it light and airy? Over time you will begin to know the difference.

Sit still for a moment. Feel the energy around your third eye, from left to right, and spin or scan the energy around you. Ask: "What am I not wanting to see or perceive, hear, feel or say in this moment?"

Imagine a spinning disc cutting diagonally through your third eye area, reaching just a little further out to the sides of your head. Now imagine the color of this energy as indigo – or you can also keep it neutral and make it from variations of luminous light in the metallic range. Spin, spin, spin away, this will clear the heaviness of the day.

HEART CHAKRA

Place both hands in the middle of your chest, overlapped not intertwined. Then place one hand over the other symmetrically and begin to feel the rise and fall of your heart.

BREATHING

Close your eyes and begin to slowly breathe in through the nose and exhale with an open mouth, expelling the air. Feel your heart. Is it rising out of your chest? Does it feel tight? Are you even able to access your breath in this area? You may find this is an area that needs strengthening, but persist in your observation and experience of just sitting with your breath for a few minutes. Do you have a shallow breath? Do you feel relief when you breathe deeply, or is it hard for you to slow it down and get into your body? Discover who you are by tuning into your body and its natural tendencies.

MASSAGE YOUR CHEST AND FEET DAILY

We can empower our lives by taking all things into our heart; then they are no longer a threat outside of us, but something we can heartfully embrace. One by one, place these people/places/situations there and imagine cleansing yourself of the hurt, hatred resentment or pain from these interactions. Imagine a washing machine in your heart; you're going to wash away the pain, cleansing yourself and others, adding the soap of forgiveness and acceptance.

Use your funnel to drain the murky water into the earth.

Massage the reflexology points in your feet and give yourself a head massage to open the channels and better connect to who you are.

EXERCISE DAILY FOR A WEEK:

Sit quietly for a few moments each day for one week and conjure people, places and situations that need your forgiveness, things that are holding you in a painful place; resentments, injustices, judgments of people's behaviors.

Take one week and ask, forgive, wash and release the water to the earth, and then once you've reconciled with each person, you can then release them and the situation down your funnel grounding cord.

AURA AWARENESS

Chakra spin: Call in the angels for assistance. Affirmation Statement: I call upon my angels, guides and guardians to guide and lead me to my highest good in all areas of my life. Bring me people, places and situations that support the enfoldment of my life in a graceful, blissful and fulfilling way for the highest best. I am open to receive inspiration and signs as a verification of my communication with the Divine. I send the light ahead and I ask that the highest will be done. I let go and trust that whatever it is I am experiencing throughout the day has been Divinely orchestrated because I called upon my support team of angels. I know that sprit is always moving me toward my desired outcome. I find the joy in all that I experience even when it gets hard and I have resistance to my circumstances. I trust my guidance.

5

VICTIMHOOD / BLAME GAME / RESISTANCE

"Our deepest fear is not that we are inadequate. Our deepest fear is that we are powerful beyond measure. It is our light, not our darkness that most frightens us. We ask ourselves, 'Who am I to be brilliant, gorgeous, talented, fabulous?' Actually, who are you not to be? You are a child of God. Your playing small does not serve the world. There is nothing enlightened about shrinking so that other people won't feel insecure around you. We are all meant to shine, as children do. We were born to make manifest the glory of God that is within us. It's not just in some of us; it's in everyone. And as we let our own light shine, we unconsciously give other people permission to do the same. As we are liberated from our own fear, our presence automatically liberates others."

~Marianne Williamson

You're the only one you have to please!

All too often we live our life to please someone else. What drives us to want to please another before pleasing ourselves?

We are a driven society. Our main goals in life are to have a lot of sex, money, fame, approval etc., and in order to attain this, many of us resort to ass kissing as opposed to loyal, truthful, sincere sharing. Our ass-kissing ways have led us to compromise our own principles to make another feel worthy, valued or loved, in order to be valued ourselves. Many of us run around pleasing others so that we don't feel guilty about being less than we are. We believe that if everyone else is happy, we'll be happy too – but this is never the case. In fact once we become professional pleasers, it's never enough. We can never do enough to make someone happy. There will always be a time where someone will want more and find fault with our behavior.

So in order to remedy this situation, you must become equipped to manage the ups and downs; you must come to know that you are ultimately the source and cause of every interaction. When you understand that every interaction is providing opportunities for you to finely tune your instrument to an empowered loving state of accepting what is, you can refocus on the experience you choose to have and feel.

Competition or Celebration - living in balance

We suffer as a society because we compete and invalidate each other's abilities. What is the motivation behind competition?

By nature, since the beginning of time, we are competing to be the best at what we do. Sport is our best example of this, because sport is so revered in our society. We teach our children that healthy competition builds character; that healthy competition gives us motivation to strive to be the best in what we do. In many ways this is a wonderful way to give people motivation to work on developing a committed practice with a focused intention. However the counter of that is, we don't always know our limits; we don't always know when enough is enough. This leads to everything becoming a competition or a fight to prove our value and worth – and what's worse, we belittle and diminish others in their efforts, rather than applauding them. Celebrate – don't player hate; you can choose what reality you play in. It's easy to understand the benefits of competitive sports and the character building that comes with creating relationships based on teamwork; but the flip side of the coin can't be ignored. Winning isn't everything and celebrating the team is what's important; acknowledging that no matter the final result, you have collaborate and participated together. In this way, YOU realize your value and worth and YOU give yourself the significance you seek. Comparing yourself to another, and to another's path and process will never be gratifying – we all have our own timelines, and so many factors come into play when participating in this game of life. So why not live a life of celebration? Because when you celebrate the achievements of others you are ultimately celebrating your own empowerment and upliftment. Ultimately we must balance out the scales and live a life that directs us toward self-love; we can do this when we understand that all interactions serve us, and we can choose to be a good sport about it.

Trust in yourself....

Experiencing a trustworthy life comes from an understanding that you influence your reality on many levels; you are drawing on so many multiple realities, past and present, from the seen to the unseen.

But where is the proof, that this reality is multi dimensional?

Take the child who trusts an authority figure, and gets violated. Or the person who thought they were safe and then experienced something unpleasant.

How could this happen to them? Because we are the sum total of our trials, tribulations joys and highs.

I have had many distinct occurrences where I felt violated and walked away thinking, how could this have happened to me? Thank god for my intuition that told me to leave and not be involved any further. Many things could have happened had I stayed, including physical rape. Two similar experiences made me come to understand that everyone is part of my evolution. I attracted these people into my life to reflect my need for love, and my pattern of looking for love on the outside. In the end, I was able to let everyone off the hook for my need for this deep desire for love and approval; I could see that these people came to show me the lesson. As I learned, I realized I could choose to no longer attract them in; that I have a CHOICE.

Why is self-trust an important navigator on your path forward? How often do we hear someone say, "I don't trust him or her", and then base future responses from this judgment? The fact of the matter is we are a co-creative universe, and trust is merely a result of what we believe in. If you are suspicious, then you are emitting that into your field; you will then attract people who act suspiciously.

No one can betray your trust if you are able to see the divine order in all things and you understand that we are what we experience in some form. The trust we seek is in our relationship with our creator and ourselves. This will be the most trusting relationship you will ever need; from there, you will automatically know that the people you encounter are merely part of your belief system, inviting you to look deeper inside to see where you can strengthen qualities within in you.

If you were in an agreement with the universe that every relationship was here to serve, benefit and grow you, then no matter the circumstance – the betrayal or the hardship – you would understand there is a higher force working on your behalf. If you blame others for the pain we experience, then you continue a cycle that does not allow for self-realization and empowered creation, because you will always be at the effect of others' actions. You give your power to outside circumstances, and you violate the trust agreement that god is your supply.

When someone says: "I can't trust that person" or "I don't think that person is trustworthy", they are demonstrating a lack of confidence in others. Trusted with what, I ask? With your heart? Your money? Your friendship? All of these are valid points, but why do you think it's up to them to prove themselves trustworthy? If you decide that someone is not who they claim to be – what are you really expecting from them? Do they have to demonstrate trustworthiness first before you'll interact with them? Are they to blame if they don't appear to be trustworthy to you? Or are you to blame because you needed to use your guidance system and not make them responsible for what you decided to do?

I've come to the conclusion that it doesn't matter if people are trustworthy or not, because I always have the choice whether or not to trust. Since I claim that I always attract people, places and situations that are trustworthy, then that has become my experience. I'm not expecting otherwise! I don't have a cautious eye for shady interactions. Instead I'm open to experiencing life and then I listen and observe, I feel into my experiences and I decide if I will place my trust on my intuition, not onto another being's life.

I trust myself and that is enough.

If I leave trust in other people's hands, then I may feel victimized. All agreements are co-operative and I may learn later that what I trusted in wasn't what I thought or expected – but that doesn't make it their fault, nor did they fail me. I am at CAUSE in the exchange and I attracted it in so I could learn valuable lessons and be more independent and trust the process of life – not to entrust more in others, but to invest that trust in myself and the direction I seek.

I am the creative controller of my destiny – no one else is. So it's up to me to align my energy in the direction of my desires and then know that no one owes me anything – not even trust. Trust for me is implied in all I do because I don't feel that I cannot trust. This is of itself a self-fulfilling prophecy. Trust not in others; trust in the Divine Will working in your favor to beget the actions and responses you seek in life for the highest good of all intended.

Trust in spirit to guide you to those opportunities that will open the way for you in every area of your life. Trust yourself. If you want to have trust and be trusted you must be the trust you seek. Trust begins with you.

In the past, when I've shared with a friend, and I trusted that they wouldn't repeat what they heard, and they did...well, I trusted that it was all for the best. And if I hadn't said anything about needing confidentiality, then all sharing is fair game. It does not make a person bad because they can't keep a secret – it doesn't mean that they want to harm you, it just means that people share as they are inspired to do so, and sometimes even when asked not to! We have to trust that the information being exchanged needed to be leaked somehow, that there was something Divine in the gossip, in the misuse of information, and it will always serve you in the end. We've seen over and over again in the media how a person can go from being the apple of our eye, to lower than low...but the beauty is that we trust and regain that trust over time, and whatever anyone has done, terrible as it might seem, they are still worthy of forgiveness.

We are like those who have failed, pick themselves back up again and succeeded. If they can do so, so can you; and this is the inspiration for all of us to want for others what we want for ourselves. My success is your success. Trust life, trust the flow, trust yourself, trust in god and you will always feel like a winner.

Trust in the process. When we trust ourselves we can trust to be delivered the correct experience for our growth knowing we are receiving Divine guidance.

Reinforcement is sought by all

You are no more special than the next person – we all have the same core needs for survival. My girlfriend was very upset that the ideas she had shared with her boyfriend were now being played back to her in a poem he had composed. She was livid that he took her material, used it and put his name on it, as if it had originated from him. Others often took the credit for her ideas, and she was angry and upset that others used her wisdom and inspiration and shared it as if it were their own. But the truth is, nothing is ours! We all have our own interpretation of the same wisdom – we just express it differently, we put our unique take on it, and then we look for acclaim for the inspiration that moves through us. We're all looking for positive reinforcement to stroke our ego. We all want to be seen for our abilities, big or small. My friend was the same; she was struggling with the need to be reinforced and acknowledged and she was buying into the idea that anyone can take anything from you. But again, nothing is ours!

Even the most humble of us still seek acclaim.

Even a nun has talents that go unwitnessed and unappreciated and, although her humility may say otherwise, even if she is not seeking reinforcement from another human her goal is to be the epitome of perfection for god. The representations of god that give the reinforcement are other humans. So we are still in search of it and we cannot surpass our human nature to be seen as wonderful beings of amazement.

No act can ever truly be selfless because there is always gratification in performing that act. We all seek this significance, even if it is just to know for our ourselves our own value and worth; we look to god or others to validate what we are. The greatest validation visibly for me is that people interact with each other and bring their love friendship and reinforcement.

Love the act of giving

Don't be fooled: giving is the same as receiving – we all have something to gain. It's hard not to feel the satisfaction of sharing; it lights people up inside and isn't this really what we want to reinforce? Igniting the torch of joy, vibrancy, meaning and approval in everyone we meet? A glance, a smile, a nod of recognition to say: I see you as a perfect child of the Creator. We are the same, we all have things to overcome, we all have unique talents and ways of being – but we are the same. I love you for being you, for having the courage to rise and share the day. I reinforce all that you are by reinforcing myself and acknowledging my godliness, my greatness. It is not your responsibility to recognize me – I see myself and because I see me, then it is obvious that I can be seen for what I truly am.

We all have qualities of divinity; for some it's only a few layers under the surface, while for others it may be buried deep, but like anything that has much soil over it, it just takes longer to dig up. And in this life, that's all we have until we pass: time to dig things up, plant seeds, wait, grow and flourish. Everything has life force and in order to thrive, it needs sun and water. After I spoke with my girlfriend and she realized she was hurt because what she wanted was recognition, she realized she needed to recognize herself in all her majesty and talents. She saw that not being recognized and rewarded for her talents doesn't change what is. She began to take great pride in who she was, and that is all that matters. At the end of the day the only relationship you have that will feed back to you who you are, is the relationship you have with yourself, and the creative source. It is up to you to how you feel with yourself; others will always judge, but god loves unconditionally and always, so snuggle closely to your Creator and the reinforcement you seek will soon be a thing of the past, as you begin to recognize yourself as that powerful source of creation.

The Five C's: compassion, cooperation, creation, courage, and communication

We're always creating more opportunities to expand into our true nature. Expanding into our true nature needs these five C's.

Every day is a breeding ground for becoming who we want to be. Life is opportunity awaiting when you awaken to the love that is awaiting your acknowledgement. However, this path of waking up to your true nature requires a deep commitment; it requires courage to stay true to yourself; it requires daily compassion for yourself and others; it needs clear communication and a willingness to make uncomfortable changes in your choices.

Over the years I've found that you can't expect another to do unto you, unless they know how to do unto themselves first. I was not able to be compassionate to others for many years because I did not feel I was worthy of it. I saw my life as an error; I was a constant mistake in action, therefore in theory compassion was nice, but not for a person who was always beating themselves up and who couldn't find the silver lining at the end of the day. It took me years to learn to love myself and therefore exhibit the same courtesy unto others.

So the first thing to remember is: do you have the capacity to do what you're asking others to do? And if you don't, then how can you expect others to mirror to you what you are not? Life is constantly giving us reflections and it's up to you to become what you ask of another. Lead by example. If I'm asking you to be more loving and compassionate then maybe I need to ask myself where I'm not being loving and compassionate to myself or to others. In order to get a hug you have to give or offer a hug. Life is mutual reciprocity, but so often we're asking for the very thing we're withholding. So pause and ask yourself: Am I complaining about something that I don't give to myself?

Be the initiator of the action; if you want to experience leadership be the leader. If we sit by idly and complain about waiting and wanting we have two choices: either be the bigger person and give what you are wanting to receive or back away. Let the universe coordinate on your behalf ingenious ways of understanding the bigger picture and allowing for the object of your desire to materialize without the attachment to when, who or where. Keep your eye on the ball and the game will be played wherever you go.

Compassionate communication comes from the ability to know what it is you're wanting from any given situation. If you're wanting peace and you're using heavy artillery, then peace may be a long ways off! But if you focus on creating peace instead of fighting for peace, you'll find you don't have to keep slinging pot shots at others. You'll begin to share what is at the source of your pain and you allow others to share what they feel about your experience. When one party begins with: "you did this" and the other defends, it becomes a battle of defense and attack. But what if you were to hear what the other person had to say and you didn't personalize it? And what if you were able to honestly admit your humanness and 'fess up to whatever perceived error you made? You wouldn't have to defend your position and you could focus your attention on finding a solution to the problem.

For example: My father has a knack for always saying the most hurtful thing to me. His erudite use of language is beyond me and the way I like to hear things is not how he articulates his message. The intention behind all he says and does comes from a place of love and wanting to see me thrive and receive the life I desire, but his delivery can feel very assumptive, critical and rude.

Once, we were talking about a breakup I was going through, and instead of compassionately saying, "Ah, I understand your feelings are hurt and you're oversensitive right now, and you may be acting in an emotional way and being too assertive because you're needy for love and attention" he said this instead: "Well maybe the reason you always experience breakups is because you're so pushy in life!" I guarantee that this was not what I wanted to hear, nor did I receive it well. It completely hurt my feelings and I was in awe of my father's lack of compassion for me. Now in hindsight I saw what he was really trying to say was: "I love you, and if the characteristics that I view to be flawed are part of your relationship with men, well maybe this is the problem; and since I want to see you happy, if you correct this you will be happier with others."

I know my father means well and in his very untactful way he points out my weaknesses and launches them in my face. The saving grace for me is to remember that all anyone wants is to be loved and approved of, and to be accepted as they are. We are all just doing our best. My father wants the best for me, and if he says hurtful things it's not to hurt me, it's to ALERT me to his perception of why my life isn't picture-perfect. What he fails to realize is that I don't need to blame my flaws on another for what I have or don't have – I just need to continuously be aware of what I can do to create better relationships, and then do more of that.

When a person is saying hurtful things, it's always good to see if there is any relevance in what they're saying. I am and have been a very pushy person; that being said, those 'flaws' have been an asset at times, because I have never given up or gone under. These are the BENEFITS to my pushiness. But this strength can equally be a detriment, pushing away the very thing I long for. So it's a fine balance, finding that winning combination and knowing when to use those dualistic qualities, and in what context. There are so many reasons why relationships do not move forward, but we can't get caught up in the minor details or the story. It takes two to tango and if you're willing to meet yourself in the reflection of the other, then the relationship will move forward. Things play themselves out in time and if the lesson is not learned here, rest assured it will repeat somewhere else. So if you have the opportunity to learn the lesson with someone, learn it and move on together. If you walk away and you haven't corrected that energy inside yourself, it will show up again in the next relationship. Do it now! And remember, it's not personal – it's reflective.

Compassionate communication is taking into consideration all sides and knowing what it is you are desiring. To avoid blowouts and blow-ups you must have a commitment to love above all, and to find the love in the opposition. It's not about forcing another to be different; it's about accepting what's happening. If you are committed to resolving the problem, then you can do it with the other, but it's not always necessary.

I'm at my pushiest when I'm looking for an outcome. I want to know the rhyme and reason behind it all – the ins and outs; what I did; what they did; and what went wrong. Unfortunately not everyone wants resolution! In fact when you strike a chord in someone, they may want to walk away. Initiating agreements and compassionate communications may work, but if it doesn't, at what price will you push for what you want? Sometimes it's better to let the other not be OK, and let them find resolution later. Sometimes being insistent on resolution has allowed situations to spin out of control in my life, because the stakes are so high. It's do or die for me, and I'm not a quitter – I'll fight till the end.

I've never understood why anyone would ever want to intentionally harm another with mean, malicious words, but I realize that no one can ever hurt another who doesn't already feel hurt. A lifetime of not being able to express their needs and having the other person receive what they're saying in love, ends up in retaliation. When two people can't hear each other, it's usually an escalation of overwhelm and years of pain and anger. How do we find a way to love when we've decided to make another pay? If you can't find what it is you're truly wanting, then how can you achieve what you want? It's not personal and when we are in a reactive state we want the other to feel the pain we feel so we persecute and punish with our words and sometimes our actions.

I resolve to have peace in all areas of my life, to live from my heart and assume that everyone is doing their best. When I don't need another's love, then I can show up and receive whatever it is they are willing to share, without expectation or disappointment. It's only when I need you to fulfill something inside of me that is dependent on your actions or inactions that I suffer. If I can just be OK with what is, then confrontation can be averted. How do we get our needs met when we're in the midst of needing? It's tricky because if you're a person who is impulsive and reactive, then your need will take precedence over the end result. Your need can be all consuming, and the spite and anger, the feeling of being victimized, can overthrow all rational thought. Then the energy system malfunctions and there's no going back. Words are flung left and right and you may not even be aware of the insanity that is coming forth. "We've been high jacked."

Tools are crucial in these times of fury or the cost can be overwhelming to all parties. Stop. Breathe. Check your ego. Can you just let go and surrender? Can you decide to respond differently? This takes strength, to ask yourself to stop being reactive to another. I've often exploded consciously, saying, "enough is enough, I want this all to stop!" and I blow up and the truth comes pouring out. There is no right way to getting your point across, but there are more peaceful ways that will get you what you want in cases of aversion, resistance, etc. If all you experience is yourself, and you can influence your reality in any given moment, then you can quickly reset and ask: Is what I'm about to fight for worth losing my joy and self worth over? You may find it's a costly price to pay to defend your wounds. If the situation can be avoided, then perhaps all your concerns can be mediated at another time when both parties are calm, when both parties can willingly interact and hear the other, not from a place of defense and victimhood, but from a place of empowerment and acceptance.

What to do when what you're wanting is not being given to you. Since life is an honor, you want to have enough self-respect not to beg. It's an honor to share, so if someone says no, then say "thank you" and walk away. Begging for it and putting the other under duress is never satisfying, because when you finally get what you want, it still hurts because it didn't come as an offering, it came from pressure.

You always have a choice

Every day you are presented with choices. What happens to your life when you understand you are the controller of your destiny by the choices you make now?

You are the captain of your ship, you decide when to set sail, when to stop and drop anchor and just be, or you navigate and move forward until you arrive. Now there may be many wonderful places you can stop and see; you can drop anchor from port to port, all the while knowing where you're headed – if so, enjoy the ride! As you do ride the wave, you confront what's there, new, in every moment. It becomes automatic once you know you're always on board and that the joy of the ride doesn't always come from arriving at your destination – it's the ride itself. If every breath you took was to be your last, you would perhaps pay attention to the people, places and situations that matter most, that are right in front of you – so seize the moment and breathe life in to the fullest.

How many of you love to get in your vehicle and take a joy ride to see the sights, or take in some fresh air, to feel the freedom one of being behind the wheel? Life is this joy ride, and encountering smoothly paved streets and the pot holes makes for an interesting time. So often I encounter people who feel they are being pressured, compromised, or hurt by others' actions. Yes, this is their real experience based on their perception of what reality is. But it takes a wise person to step up and realize: YOU are in the driver's seat and what you are experiencing is just that – an experience, YOU give it value and meaning.

Yes, it would be amazing to be able to control everything and everyone around us, in order to avoid ever feeling less than a perfect child of god – but how much fun would that be? You'd know what to expect at every turn, and life would become monotonous. The beauty of life is we have free will to co-create and we are free thinkers. We are presented with choice all day long. What to eat, what to wear, where to buy gas, where to live, where to go to school, who to hang out with, will you put your right shoe on first or your left, will you wash your hair today. It's non-stop – so when someone says they don't feel like they have a choice, it's not true! All they have are choices!

Even children make choices, from the moment they enter into earthly form. They co-create with their parent/s when to eat, when to bathe, when to cry, when to move. Voluntarily or involuntarily, it's happening.

So here's the thing: PAY ATTENTION! Wouldn't it be wise to bring attention to what you can consciously create, when new material presents itself in front of you? And how about re-evaluating the things we do routinely? Ever consider doing it differently or changing your perceptions or even changing your ways? We choose to stay, we choose to go; no one can obligate us and if we feel we are being imposed upon, forced, threatened or harmed, we can do one of two things. We can choose a new direction or surrender into what we are experiencing as an opportunity for expansion and understanding.

Self-realization and growth is the understanding that we are always moving forward in some fashion. Even if we repeat the same thing over and over again, it will never be done the same way twice – it's impossible, as every moment is unique onto itself. So what does choice provide? It provides a mechanism to become self-liberated, self-sovereign.

Now let's take an example. A woman has two children and a husband who she describes as "emotionally unavailable. She's unhappy; she craves freedom and intimacy. What should she do? She could go outside the marriage to get her needs met; she could leave him; she could go for couples therapy and address her needs; she could stay and complain and make herself miserable because she feels trapped, obligated, scared to be on her own. So many choices, right? And there is no one, right, choice. All are viable. All are valid.

Now, depending on your intentions in life, depending upon your foundational value system, and your belief-set, your response is based on what you've learned. But are you willing to see it another way? What if up 'til now, everything you thought to be true was the opposite? You would see that there is only self-responsibility. What you need and desire or demand from the outside world can only come to you once you've understood that it's up to you to draw that into your experience. What you may perceive as punishment may be the very thing to motivate you to take immediate action towards something new and previously unseen.

Let's go deeper. So you realize: OK, I have a choice, but with all these responsibilities, how can I manage my past choices, so I can navigate through future choices? Well, the beauty is that everything is being divinely designed to serve you. Once again, it's not only about arriving at your destination but also enjoying yourself along the way. I've been a traveller since I was 14 and I'd say some of the most profound experiences I've had was while I was in transit.

You decide: what is your life going to look and feel like; you design the plan. You will get what you look for. Ever played the game, 'Where's Waldo?' Eventually you'll find him, if that's your quest. So the key is to not make the journey or the participants wrong along the way. On your journey, stay curious, see what appears before you. The universe is always waiting to surprise you – but only if you believe that. It's not what you do, it's how you feel about the things you do that gives rise to choices that are supportive.

I was dating a man who insisted on being respected. This doesn't even factor into my vocabulary, but I understood the meaning of his request. However I found it was not something I wanted to give, not did I ever know if I were giving it or not! Based on his value system and how he felt about himself, he was always going to attract a women like me, to disrespect him, because we can only give and receive what we already have for ourselves. If you respect yourself, the other will respect you – and vice versa. I was the perfect match for his law of attraction – and of course, he served me immeasurably too, so I could see and understand myself more deeply. The people who are not seeking respect are usually the ones commanding it and having it.

So I this relationship, I connected with my father, who always asked for respect. I used to think, well, if you want respect, shouldn't you be giving it? If either of these men had self-respect (which equals self-love) then they wouldn't be asking me to respect them, and I wouldn't even come into their field of attraction. So now I have to ask myself: if everything is a reflection and everyone has choice, what am I doing to call this in? How am I being? So then I realize, oh yes, I want to control how they see me, because I am influenced by their opinion of me; I have give away my power because I am looking to them, and not within myself, for the validation I need that says I'm worthy and lovable. Then I saw how I also want to be understood; and that must feel like not being respected feels to them!

Now let's go deeper.

So then I realized: if I understood that I can only control myself and my perception of what I experience, then it would no longer be necessary to seek understanding from another. So I would cease seeking understanding (or respect) from others since I am the captain of the ship and I decide how to navigate my machinery. Then there would be no blame on the other person and no one would ask you to behave differently to accommodate their needs - they would show up self realized and actualized as deliberate creators of their own reality. So the point is: we all have a choice to engage or walk away; if we decide to stay and play and it doesn't go our way, that too is beneficial, because we get to see what we'd like to experience next.

Is life easy and peaceful or a constant fight and a war? The person who says I don't fight is probably the biggest fighter, because asking to be, or avoiding what ails you, is what will draw it to you. I know better than anyone from my constant insistence about my sensitive ways and getting everyone to accommodate me, rather than me adapting to a new mind-set that would lead to my living a balanced life of extra sensory perceptions that are manageable and supportive. I am still refining this today, how to upgrade my own self-imposed ways.

We find what we seek. We create what we focus on. We choose how to define our experiences as good or bad, but the truth is: it's just what it is – just notice how it makes you feel.

If you stopped qualifying all of your choices as good or bad, and you just experienced life, then you would know that at any given moment, you could walk out of a situation that did not fall in line with your highest purpose. You could stop fighting. Or blaming. You could let everyone off the hook.

You choose.

Go with the flow and see where it takes you. Stop asking others to accommodate you and adjust by taking inventory and evaluating your behavior. That way, you won't need to complain and explain, you'll liberate yourself – and you will be the change you want to see.

Life is an honor not an obligation.

How can we live our lives in the choice of honor rather than obligation? I grew up with a father who felt the burden of obligation thrust upon him. Later in life I tried to understand how a man with so much could feel like he had so little. How could he not see that these obligations were really beautiful opportunities to improve on how he managed himself and the world around him?

When we take a vow in marriage, we are claiming a new state of being; we step into a contract and this shifts how we feel about the person we are choosing to unite with. The irony is that once those vows are exchanged something else shifts, and it's usually your perception of what freedom means! Now I've heard my father complain about all his obligations – his children! – And in my mind I say to myself, you made the choice to have 5 children, and yes, there are responsibilities that come with that choice. So instead of complaining, see the opportunities you've been given to share your life with them, and others.

Blessings in disguise

There are always hidden meanings behind why we experience what we experience. How can we uncover the subtext of these hidden meanings? By taking a daily inventory, discovering who we are and how we feel about what we're experiencing. Most people have a check in point daily – a child may check in with a parent, or an adult with a full-time job has to clock on and off, to give accountability for their time. We do this out of habit, so let's do it intentionally, on an internal emotional level.

When something went wrong, and then worked out in the end, we've probably all said, "That was a blessing in disguise!" And when we connect the dots, we truly know that we had been led down that particular path. If it hadn't been for xyz, I wouldn't be here now...

That's when you really know that life's little irritants can be your greatest blessings. Today in yoga, my teacher told us a story about a man who encountered everything with the words: "lets wait and see". A neighbor would say, "How fortunate is this!" and another would say, "How unlucky is that," to which he would always respond, "Lets wait and see". My teacher said, what can seem unfortunate can be an unforeseen blessing. Life will always teeter-totter in both directions, let's get back into that playfulness where we can love the ups and downs and can embrace what is. That's the beauty of living in a body – we get to have all experiences!

You are the center stage and it's your show

All we experience is ourselves. The universe revolves around us...so how do we understand ourselves in our experiences?

How many yous are there, and how can they all co-exist?

We have so many faces and personalities, how can we accept them and ourselves?

We all have many personalities and they are all wanting attention; they all raise their heads at various times, so how do we manage this? People often associate anger and rage as undesirable emotions but what I've been taught is, we are this energy in motion (Emotion). So in order to live in harmony with all these personalities, we have to give them a voice. I say let them take center stage and perform! Stop pushing them behind the curtain! Once they've completed their performance, they've been seen and heard and experienced, and they will cease to cause harm and pain, blending back into the neutral energy that co-exists with all your other emotions.

Emotions hold no value – they just are what they are – and when they rise, let them raise so high that they evolve into the realization that there is expressive beauty. Here's an example: You're working steadily and a child of 3 or 4 comes in screaming and yelling, trying to get your attention. If you keep shoving that child away, I can guarantee after the 3rd blood-curdling scream you'll probably turn to them to see what's happening. Now since I care about the words I use, I say, "what's happening" not "what's wrong" – there's no need to imply there is a wrong.

The child explains that his little friend next door has destroyed his toy, given to him by a beloved family member. A fight ensues, because frustration has arisen. You listen to that child, you love, you nurture, and then the child, having been heard, goes off to play. A moment ago, they were a whirlwind of energy in motion; they felt, they expressed, they overcame and they moved into being their full expression of love. The child would never judge itself for being a child, because a child just expresses what it experiences. But as adults we have a different opinion of ourselves when we behave that way; we belittle, we judge, we shame, we make guilty, we store and file this incident as a marker of how unlovable we are. Emotion (energy in motion) is just that – so when we allow ourselves to feel our feelings we are remembering to be like the child. Of course, if we outwardly act like a child, others will judge us as being childish! The trick is to experience like a child, without giving voice to what's happening inside.

We have to be genuine and get real with what we feel – only then will we find liberation and be able to accept what is, without placing a value judgment on whether it's right or wrong.

The universe does revolve around you! All you experience is yourself. You may feel what others feel, however you are the one feeling it, by proximity or by empathy; once you perceive it and feel it, it becomes yours. I've found though my own de-layering process that I've identified myself with certain emotions and although I felt I had traversed these emotions, I was still being affected by others who had a similar vibration. Mine first felt like a pebble and theirs was like a mountain – but when I was done with the exchange, mine turned into the mountain! I resisted this because I'd blame them, saying, "Well, I didn't feel this until I went deeply into your pain and now I can only feel your pain!' The only way I could come into love again was to embrace the feeling and see where I still related to this pain. So in order to traverse the pain I had to go in and remember what's real and current and then surround myself in love. That might be to surround myself with people I love or to hike or do yoga – whatever it is, I immerse myself into that, knowing that I am not separate from my experience and that it's just an experience.

The feeling then dissipates because I understand that emotions are constantly in flux and are just energy in motion. My point of reference is to always go home to my heart and feel what comes in to my experience; I know that if I deny, reject or push it away, it persists. So I surrender; I inquire; I let the emotions rise to the surface; I give them center stage; and I look deep within. Once the feelings are felt, then I go and play. I switch my focus to something that reminds me of the love that I am. I am renewed and reset to experience play just like the child, for whom everything is new in every moment.

Blame game of pain

Is life a place of victimization or creation?

It's up to you how you manage your encounters. We are so used to being in this victim /perpetrator paradigm that we don't even know we're doing it on the most subtle levels. When you feel that another is imposing on your life, or making you feel bad, or manipulating you into guilt for not being what they want, then you know you've hit the jackpot! You're officially playing the blame game!

Well – if you're going to do it, then be the best at it! Do it with love, or don't do it all.

If you took on the attitude that everything you encountered was beneficial to you; that everything on your path comes to you because you are emitting a vibration of what you truly, subconsciously believe, then you may find that some of those buried fears aren't so buried! They may be looming in the distance to be addressed and handled from a new perspective. If you continue basing your future based on the past, you will certainly achieve and receive your past. It's an inclusive universe – what you put your attention on will emerge, expand and become more and more apparent. It's like being an anthropologist or archaeologist, but what you're uncovering are your own skeletons and remnants of the past that you have stored within. Time to excavate and see what's there! Is it current with who you are and who you want to become? Are these remnants weighing you down, keeping you locked in fear? Is it time to give a proper, loving burial to what you've known in order to rebirth it into whom you are today? In order to discover what you are. You have to willing to uncover who you were, with love and acceptance, knowing that it led you to this moment of NOW.

We all do it; we all love to blame someone else for our pain. It could be a little innuendo like saying, "Hey, if you had told me you were cancelling, I would have done something else!" And you huff and sigh in angst and frustration, rather than thanking that person for liberating you to find your way to something else; a something else that is more likely than not a better choice for you!

We are instinctual beings and we all have a GPS (god-powered-system) inside of us navigating the path ahead. Are you following your instincts? Often times we're living from the perception of what we perceive to be right or wrong, and we appease others rather than really meeting our own needs, moment to moment. Only by listening to your inner voice can you know yourself and make adjustments. It takes courage to live in this expanded state of being with the what is, noticing what shows up and then moving into a place of trusting that god will supply the ultimate ride to the other side.

In order to evolve past blame and shame, and play a new game, you must take full responsibility for your actions to date and see how even your thoughts contributed to the events that transpired; your thoughts manifested into form. What you focus on will always expand and come into form. Fear can become your best friend as long as you stay attentive; listen to it when it appears, then tune in to see what is true and what is an old story. It's always easier to run away than it is to stay and be love.

All you experience is yourself and when you encounter what you don't like in another, it gives you the opportunity to see if you like it in yourself. Most of the times the things that unnerve us, that we are intolerant of, are a by-product of the need to control our environment in order to feel safe. If we were to know once again we were always right where we needed to be, and that we were safe, then we may experience another reality. Under the laws of god and grace we are never wrong, we are just under the illusion that we are separate from source. Once we reconnect with source, we enter the flow. There is always rhyme and reason to what we experience. This is my model of the world and this is what works for me. I tried it the other way and I can falter and forget and still dabble in the victim / perpetrator consciousness, but it never feels as empowering and as uplifting as when come back to source and act as a loving, compassionate being toward myself first and foremost, honoring my feelings and needs without judgment, I nurturing myself at the pace of grace. You can't sit in embarrassment for what you were! Move forward and be flexible and live your life toward what you know is possible. Let go and let god.

Victim consciousness is embedded in and around us, and we are so blind to it that we don't even know how it's affecting us. No one is exempt from the massive media affront on our culture and lifestyle. It's almost impossible to drive down the street and not be affected by what you see – marketing strategies that subliminally coerce you, the consumer, into believing that by buying a product, you can reinforce your self-worth or improve your self image.

That's why it's so important to know yourself; so important to have a strong foundation of understanding to the truth about whom you are. It is also vital to know that god is in all things and that whatever you support you become a part of that consciousness. So where are you directing your funds, time and attention? Ultimately there is never a wrong choice – only learning – but the average person is unable to pay attention to the signs. We have stunted our creativity and we have stopped questioning what is the most correct experience for every individual. Instead marketers appeal to the masses, and the masses are grossly unaware of the organic reality of this world. We have become a plastic consuming culture of misinformed individuals who give our power away to the wind. Education is imperative – to our nation, to our soul, to our hearts. We have forgotten the heart and soul of it all. I am here to awaken and remind us that what we do for one we do for all – so it begins with you. Your contribution is what we need, so you must become aware of the environment, personally, globally and locally. But first and foremost it begins with the people you encounter on a daily basis.

We have an awesome opportunity to create our every moment, to create the lives we want. This takes dedication, motivation, imagination, and the heart of a child. To live the dream we must see the dream and then hold our focus upon the realization of that dream. So often we have a dream and we awaken excited, ready to activate it – and then we get caught up in the reality of what is. We get lost in the past, forlorn about the future and oh so quickly, the dream fades and we encounter our perception of a nightmare…daily life. Are you choosing to live the dream or fuel the fire of the undesired, unfulfilling nightmare? It takes resilience, faith and dedication to remain on track and see through the stormy nights, knowing that the rain will eventually end, and when the last drop has fallen, a freshness permeates the air, there is a newness to life, the skies are clear, and the sun comes out to kiss us and bestow blissfulness. This life can be all that we want it to be – or it can be all that we don't want. It's your choice.

I have become a living testament to creating my reality. I always create what I focus on. I've realized throughout the years that I have been challenged in maintaining self-love; therefore I am always the first to prove myself a failure way before anyone else can – yet I persevere. I came to realize that all the years I complained about what I didn't want, I was creating just that – what I didn't want! I was not savvy to "The Game of Life", so named in Florence Scovel Shinn's book from the 1920's; I didn't know that language was a large component of my destructive, repetitive patterns. I was only aware of my focus, and this was far too often on complaining about everything, identifying that which I did not want and thereby inviting it in! I was a master of indulgence, complaints, subtle manipulation, guilt, victimhood and DRAMA – definitely my specialty! I prided myself on being the person who would attract the strangest accidents, mishaps and weird occurrences. I thrived on the drama, the attention and the pain, while all the while complaining that I wanted a happy life full of love, health and joy. But these things were never in my reality. When I did experience a little joy, I would always find a way to sabotage and leave myself feeling unworthy, abandoned, hurt, sick tired and defeated. I was a professional self-hater; I did it better than anyone I knew. In fact, if I feared that someone would dislike me, I would prove myself unworthy of love and befitting of judgment before they could! Now don't get me wrong, I've had many, many special and magical moments as well, because my heart's desires and the innocence and yearning of my soul to ascend and love myself would emerge sporadically enough to keep me going.

But as the years wore on I grew tired of turning my wheels and repeating the same story over and over and over again. The story never changed although the circumstances did, as did my location and my friends, but I replayed the same tune everywhere I went. It was an insidious reminder of my inability to cope, to be healthy and happy. My feelings of undeserving-ness weighed so heavy on my soul that I would ruin every one of my relationships because ultimately I did not feel worthy of love. I would devise excuses and little inconsequential things to complain about; I would always find what was wrong and inflate those aspects of the relationship until ultimately every man left me because I was impossible to please. I would become controlling whenever I felt afraid; I felt vulnerable, but I saw vulnerability as weak and feeble; I had to show my strength in order to maintain control of my surroundings. As long as I had control, I could handle the pain. It really wasn't my fault that every man I dated was flawed and really didn't love me and really only wanted me for my body...nook. I wasn't to blame, so I blamed my father, my brothers, my past, my mother, the mean kids at school, my lack of this that and that. I had a million and one excuses as to why I was a socially inept, flawed human being beyond repair. I was a litigator, a debater, a fighter; I defended my ego to the death.

But in the end, my heart won the war between me, myself and I. The ego was demolished, the agenda was squelched and the perceptions of unworthiness were unproven, as I learned, step-by-step what it means to be in love and how to maintain it.

We are the masters of our mind – we don't mind what the masters say, but we master what we mind! Our nemesis is doubt, fear, guilt, lack of trust, lack of self worth, our mother, our father, every man or woman who has an opinion about us. There will always be an opposing view of what is true, and it is up to you to discover what that truth is. Isn't is silly, that we let people who clearly don't love themselves determine our value and worth, when they can't even value themselves? Isn't it silly that the people we look up to have the authority over how we feel? Isn't it silly that these unknowing, self-loathing people make us who we are, by giving us our value? Yes, we have all done it; we have all given away our power to forces outside ourselves? Inferiority vs. superiority, extraordinary vs. ordinary, empowered vs. devalued. The beautiful thing about life is that we all have the same feelings and no one is exempt from experiencing them all. We may have numbed ourselves to these feelings, from years of running away, from years of fear, but we all had the same set when we started out. The mind is an amazing tool, and it is never too late to begin to access all that you are today. You are reawakening and re-birthing yourselves as the perfect individual you were born to be and you are going to re-educate yourselves on what it takes to become all that you know yourself to be.

Infinite possibilities start with the abolition of titles, judgments, stereotypes, traditions, should' woulda' coulda' living-in-the-past-projecting-into-the-future. Your life begins here and now, in this very moment. We are going to recreate every step of the way with easy principles that you can apply to your daily life regardless of what you see and believe to be your current reality.

What you resist persists

Why? It's all about focus. If you are yet to harness this skill then you will continually call into your experience the very thing you are resisting because the universe is inclusive. It will deliver to you what you are intent upon. So if you want to create a new reality you must see a new reality emerging from the now based on your present desire. The past is an excellent barometer for showing you how you've behaved to date. So if you see there are reoccurring experiences that displease you perhaps you take time to consider a new route of passage forward a new point of focus and discover what it is by allowing it to be what it was.

Only then can you create what will be from this new perspective and reality. So resist away, I'm saying RESIST because in the struggle or resistance we no longer can empower the pain of it and can see it clearly for what it is (FOCUS). It will teach you what to pay attention to. I guarantee when you release the struggle of whatever it is that ails you and you focus on something else you like or love you may find that it vanishes or it stops creating emotional turbulence for you as you've surrendered into accepting what is.

CHAPTER FIVE SUMMARY:

VICTIMHOOD / BLAME GAME / RESISTANCE

1. Celebration is the act of teamwork and camaraderie, it is the acknowledgement that no matter what the final result, you have put in the time and energy to focus upon creating an end result and that is the merit of achievement through the act of participation.

2. The fact of the matter is, we are a co-creative universe and trust is merely a result of what you believe in. No one can betray your trust if you are able to see the divine order in all things and you understand that we are what we experience in some form.

3. I am the creative controller of my destiny – no one else is. So it's up to me to align my energy in the direction of my desires and then know that no one owes me anything – not even trust. Trust for me is implied in all I do because I don't feel that I cannot trust.

4. Trust not in others; trust in the Divine Will working in your favor to beget the actions and responses you seek in life for the highest good of all intended. Trust in spirit to guide you to those opportunities that will open the way for you in every area of your life. Trust yourself. If you want to have trust and be trusted you must be the trust you seek. Trust

begins with you.

5. At the end of the day the only relationship you have that will feed back to you who you are, is the relationship you have with yourself, and the creative source.

6. Be the initiator of the action. If you want to experience leadership be the leader. If you sit by idly and complain about waiting and wanting, you have two choices: either be the bigger person and give what you are wanting to receive, or back away and let the universe coordinate on your behalf the object of your desire to materialize without the attachment to when, who or where. Keep your eye on the ball and the game will be played wherever you go.

7. It takes two to tango and if you're willing to meet yourself in the reflection of the other, then the relationship will move forward.

8. If you have the opportunity to learn the lesson with someone, learn it and move on together. If you walk away and you haven't corrected that energy inside yourself, it will show up again in the next relationship. Do it now! And remember, it's not personal – it's reflective.

9. No one can ever hurt another who doesn't already feel hurt.

10. When I don't need another's love, then I can show up and receive whatever it is they are willing to share, without expectation or disappointment.

11. I live my life from honored choice and I am always delivered the right people places and situations to expand me into the most magnificent self-realized loving me.

12. What can seem unfortunate can be an unforeseen blessing.

13. All we experience is ourselves. We have to be genuine and get real with what we feel – only then will we find liberation and be able to accept what is, without placing a value judgment on what's right or wrong.

14. If we stop making others and ourselves wrong and we go beyond, we can come into an understanding of that we all have our own value system. It isn't right or wrong, it just is, until we remodel it from empowered co-creation and focused intention.

6

RELATIONSHIPS

The people we are in relationship with are always a mirror, reflecting our own beliefs, and simultaneously we are mirrors, reflecting their beliefs. So... Relationship is one of the most powerful tools for growth.... If we look honestly at our relationships, we can see so much about how we have created them.

~ Shakti Gawain ~

"No one can make you feel inferior without your consent."
~ Eleanor Roosevelt; Former First Lady of the United States

How to get along with people who are not willing to be or do what you want.

We're so accustomed to wanting OUR way that we'll fight, insist and demand it at all costs, particularly when we have conviction about something that troubles us. We think that our way is the only way to solve what we see as a problem. As a teacher I'm always in awe of what experiences I call into my field.

Someone asked me recently: are you always happy and in high energy?

I'm always feeling and right where I need to be. My aim in life is not to achieve happiness but to achieve stillness with what is, and find resolutions that feel supportive to my commitment for understanding, expansion, self-realization and love.

Easier said than done, right? However, life is what we perceive it to be. What would life look like if you knew you were using every situation in your life to make you feel something? It's up to you to bring yourself into awareness and manage what authentically appears. "There is no Law of Assertion, just Law of Attraction." Jeff Kentner.

Does dialogue always give resolution? If you're not getting the feedback you want then resolution can feel like a distant future. So the resolution must come from within: remember, it all begins and ends with you. Hindsight is always 20/20, and it's easier to look back at what we could have said or done, or not done. The beauty of life is that we are given these opportunities to continually monitor what is before us. Do you like it? Does it support you feeling the way you want to?

It never feels good to be rejected or denied love and celebration, however if the universe is conspiring on your behalf to find the highest resolution, then you need to trust that the universe is bringing you all the right people, places and situations. In any given moment, things arise, and we are feeling beings, so we cannot prevent emotions from rising to the surface. But it's what we do afterwards to stay in a place of love and compassion in order to maintain our own positive vibration that's important.

What are you seeing? Insecurity is an awesome tool for expansion! As all your fears and pain surface, you create situations that will allow you to step up into what you really know, as opposed to what you fear.

There is no better or worse. Everyone is in his or her perfect place, and we honor the other by acknowledging that there is a path for all of us, no matter how circuitous. You might have the skills to play in the major league, but sometimes you just want to

play in the minor league, and while it might feel like a backward step, there is beauty in just playing the game at any level.

The way IN is the way out.

"IN-turn-ally" changing for a better you.

All you experience is yourself.

So develop a feedback system and be honest with what you feel is important, while at the same time honoring and identifying the source of origin. Rejection is the protection, which is the correction and the redirection, because what is FOR you comes toward you, and what is AGAINST you moves away from you.

Intimate relationships are the best illustrations of this. There's a deep love between Lucy and Chad, they love so deeply, they "fall in love" (I call it "rising in love"), they also experience pain, fighting, hurt, lack of support, contradiction, anger and sadness. This relationship becomes so reflective, they get to see their demands, and how much control they want over the other. Victimhood and blame overshadows it all. So what happened to the love? I believe we are given assignments and when the assignment is over then we move on to the next project, so to speak. This does not mean that these interactions are not meaningful because every interaction will grow you into a better you. Contrary to belief it's usually the challenge, which gives us the drive to forge forward and discover the victory. Along the way the universe provides us with many obstacles, choices and opportunities to go, do, or are anything we choose to achieve. "What you believe you can achieve." This is my interpretation of author Joseph Murphy's philosophy.

OK, so we rise in love, then we crash into pain, fear, opposition, timing, irreconcilable differences that split us, and what became one now becomes two and we move in another direction. So why do we hold on to that one experience or person? Because we all want significance, love and approval, to feel as if our life matters. We all want to feel important, to feel that we are included and are a part of something. But we're usually never satisfied, because in the moment we get what we want, we question our value or our worthiness.

How do we rise above this perpetual experience of feeling like a victim and feeling like we are never enough? It's like we have 50 of our greatest fans in one corner, cheering us on, and there's one naysayer! If we are in a state of questioning our value and worth the one naysayer will drown the cheers out. You were looking for it all along and voila, you found it! Something to invalidate you and confirm your own aberrant beliefs about your lack of self-love and recognition.

All it takes is to pivot in the direction of your desire.

In the military, the command is: "about face" – and you turn and there's a whole new view awaiting you. So move toward the 50 and let go of the one! But with the understanding that the one is just showing you a part of your consciousness, which needs love too. It also shows us that not everyone will be able to celebrate who we are, because they do not celebrate who they are. When you are committed to celebrating who you are, then the universe will definitely deliver to you the people, places and situations that support your consciousness. Everything you encounter is an extension of you. So where do you relate to the naysayer? Are you denying yourself the love and support you deserve? We all deserve the greatest love life has to offer and it starts with you.

Strategies to contend with an unhappy fan

Remember the person who starts booing were once cheering for something. Fear of the unknown can provoke many of our interactions today and can turn the friend into the enemy. There is a time and place for all things and that is why my model of BEING means being present to what IS, right now.

What are you noticing NOW? What's showing up NOW?

So the frenemy (once friend, now enemy) is our greatest gift. When we no longer resonate with the reflection before us and we start moving at a different pace, the universe will naturally move us in the direction of our focus and expand us there. I know it can feel personal and hurtful, because in relationships, especially intimate ones, we open to our fears and vulnerabilities. However love and hate are not personal! And it's your perception of these states of being that determine how you will feel about yourself. We fall (rise) in love with another because we fall (rise) in love with who we are in their presence. Its delicious and sumptuous to have someone celebrate you, to want to do for you, be there for you and include you. And the good news is when one story completes, a new story begins. We build it, we dream it, and we step into it, through it and toward it. So the way I find solace when I need to let go of something I dearly love, is to know that every experience and person is a representation of me getting closer to what I see as my vision for a fuller life for myself.

As I slough off layers of pain, I enter into more gain. As I experience life, I SEE it. I try not to repeat the same lesson, but if I do, I understand that I am creating a better outcome. If I regress completely to the old pattern of behavior, then I realize it's just an experience, and how I respond to myself in for-giving and loving what I am, is how I progress.

It's never about the other person – they are just helping you to navigate toward or away from your desired outcome.

Strategies

1. Once you've realized you're feeling victimized, choose to take a more empowered approach and see what that person

is bringing to your attention.

2. If you've experienced it before in some fashion, it's probably not about the person, but the pattern that they're showing you.

3. Uncover the source of origin – mother, father, sibling, ex. Where have you felt or experienced a similar feeling?

4. Most experiences are based on our past; we're all bringing forth-learned responses.

5. There are benefits to every experience that comes on your path. In knowing the benefit, you will be able to come into appreciation for the experience.

6. There is no right or wrong way to behave, all is par for the course of self-realization to deeper understanding and expansion.

7. You decide the protocol to how you live your life.

8. If you ask others to determine your course of action and you don't like the choices they've made for you, and you now blame them for your experience, you are in the victim/perpetrator mode. You have lost sight of the value and benefits that every experience allows you to cultivate personal power.

9. Always tune in and see if the outcome you desire feels supportive for your bigger picture, that of having interactions that inspire your expansion.

10. Take a little time and space before making rash decisions. Time can serve as an amazing buffer to having clarity and acting from an empowered place of choice and self-knowing.

11. In the moment of assault and reaction take a moment to review and see, how did it make you feel? How did someone telling me to stay away forever make me feel? How does this request benefit me to move toward my new current choice of reality?

12. There is no pushing or force, unless there is an opposing receiver of the behavior.

13. No one can treat you poorly because the standard of how you are treated is determined by how you treat yourself. No one else is to blame.

14. If you don't like what you hear – so what. It's usually delivered through that individual's filter and it isn't personal. We assert when we want to control and if we feel we can't change or control another, we may use words of offence to get our way.

15. So what if someone offends you. You decide to give words and actions 'weight' in your life. If you are only ever talking to yourself and you are only experiencing your personal version of life then you are listening with a filter and receiving messages through another's filters.

16. Perhaps your filter needs to be cleaned and you need to let go of limiting beliefs and re-evaluate, update and get current to what you choose to believe today.

17. If you go against what is and you obsess over changing someone's mind it will be an uphill battle. If you correct yourself and come into the understanding that you cannot loose what is not yours, then you know there is never a wrong way – just a way through and toward your desired destination.

18. I cannot save you or anyone from your own pain but I can promote love and help you to see that there is always fair and right action.

19. We can't always explain the source of pain; we are multi-dimensional beings and have lived many lifetimes, so many things are influencing interactions (karma, mother, father, trauma, etc.) – it's an accumulated effect. What we can do is address what it is we feel in the moment and direct our focus toward the good feelings that will neutralize what's been and get us current to what is.

20. Stepping away does not denote giving up. Follow your heart. In the avoidance of what you don't want by adhering to the rules of others, you will never win. However if you honor what appears in the name of love then choices can be made from a place of peace and stillness, even if that's to go from being a couple to a single; there is never true division and separation as we are all interconnected. So when we say farewell we say hello to the new and this could be exhilarating.

21. There are multiple entries to life, and once inside, it's your journey and your game and you call the shots. Be mindful that if you make up the rules then don't follow those rules you are guaranteed to experience them in the external world in order to see that you are out of integrity. We will

always play our own version of the game of life we've set in motion.

22. Step toward what you choose.

23. I've met many people who speak of boundaries, high values, adding value in relationships, wanting to be treated with respect, only to demonstrate the opposite. They do this because they haven't addressed the core issue, which is peaceful resolution within the self, and having compassion for people's inability to manage their emotions, responding instead in fear and limitation, imposing our rule set. So recognize when you are expecting others to do unto you what you haven't done unto yourself. If you want respect, be the epitome of respect towards yourself and others. Then the need to receive that from others will fall away as you will deeply feel that all you encounter is built upon the foundation that you have implemented for yourself.

24. It's not up to you to make me O.K. – it's up to me. If I run from you and focus on the trauma and drama that could appear then I live in fear and draw that near.

25. Can you see past the limitations of others and see their perfection, their potential realized, that they are exactly as they need to be? In the experience of withdrawal, rejection and sometimes cruelty, there is perfection in that too. We're not here to control or change others but to invite in possibilities that give life extensions into a fuller reality of love as our by-line.

26. How do you honor others' requests when they are diametrically opposing your views? Listen to your heart and live in the joy of seeing right action for all concerned.

See what appears then.

27. If you look for what's wrong, you'll find it. If you think you've done something wrong then you will find that too. There is no wrong – there is only choice. If I can't please you or my behavior offends you then you have a choice how to respond. You could blow it off, you could laugh it off, you could personalize it as an affront to you, you could say I don't relate with people who do x, y, z, and then you have your laundry list! I guarantee if that's what you want to avoid, that's what you'll find.

28. Telling another what to do – even as a parent – doesn't mean you know what's best. We are all SELFISH so when we pretend to want to protect another we are often only doing it to prevent worry for ourselves. Imposing your ideas on what you think is right and wrong inhibits the flow of life.

29. We are all guided and we all have choice but I do not have to adhere to your rule set if I feel differently. Conflict ensues when we force our way, as opposed to carve the way with freedom to create in the moment. Making promises we can't keep in order to please others or setting up a structure of limitation is just that – limited. Not inspired and usually coming from a place of fear to maintain our image that we are not vulnerable beings who feel and fall and rise again. We protect, and this protection stems from fear of being judged. We can never truly hide, the truth will always find its way to the surface even if it's just our own personal acknowledgement. We would never tell another to do or not do something when we know the universe is coordinating on our behalf right action at all times. Secrets would be a thing of the past and we would

share who and what we are and be mindful of the information being exchanged and how to best offer what we know.

30. You cannot change others, you cannot control what others will do or say. You can only learn to manage your emotional response by bringing yourself into an aware state of acceptance by being with what is and then directing your focus toward a good feeling place. This is the law of attraction in action. Be deliberate. We are creating all the time consciously and unconsciously, so the more you're aware of your internal state the more you can bring yourself into alignment with your vision

How does redemption come when we hold tightly to rules that implement a structure of separation?

I had a dear friend who spent years struggling with a man she was deeply in love with. It finally came to a head and he moved on to another woman. All the while my girlfriend was certain they would end up together so she yo-yoed back and forth in her mind, following her heart and arguing with her mind. Now the law of attraction is an amazing force to be reckoned with, as we speak out what we want and feel into what we don't want the juxtaposition of opposition will bring it all to a head. What you focus on will continue increasing.

My girlfriend specifically asked me not to say anything to her ex boyfriend who is also a friend and client of mine (now soon to be married to another woman), to not let him know that she was hurt and wanted closure. In the moment she asked, I felt coerced to agree. She shared how she felt with me, told me her story and then said – "but don't say anything!"

A few weeks later I found myself in a texting exchange with her ex-boyfriend and I mentioned my dear friend, and asked about his recent engagement. (Now I believe in celebrating people and just because one person feels wronged by an individual, it is not for me to judge or stop loving that person based on their experience. I choose to respond individually based on my guidance and personal interaction.)

I mentioned that, given his line of work as a life coach, he might like to have a conversation for closure with his ex. Now she specifically asked me not to say anything, and without any impulse control, I just couldn't help myself! My intention was for her to gain resolution, and I would be the catalyst for this resolution by being direct and telling him to mind his manners and be in integrity and give her a truthful and honest exchange. He agreed to do so and I felt satisfied and happy that I had said something to him, even though she had asked me not to. She of course, understandably was not happy! She was angry and felt that I had betrayed her trust. I thought she would forgive me but it seems that betrayal has been part of her patterning in the past, and of course, until resolved it continues to appear. I had no choice but to show up as a betrayer, given her track record. It's almost like we can't stop ourselves from doing or saying certain things, even if it we know the potential for hurt – because the other has placed rules on how we must behave in order to be loved by them. Two other friends acted in the same way, and she had drawn us all into her life pattern!

Now I love to grow. I'm curious, and as hard as it may be, I traverse many painful situations due to the fact that I really choose to be the best me, even if I don't do it according to what is deemed by others as correct. I will learn, I will grow, I will forgive and I will let go and let god. I understand the higher guiding force at play bringing to the surface all our insecurities and giving rise to loving one another in our humanity. There is no offence that is unforgiveable, because ultimately if it's happening to you there is something to gain from it for you.

On the surface, my friend told me she had forgiven me…it felt good to complete that with her. But two days later, I received a text from her stating how uneasy she felt and that she couldn't be my friend right now.

How many of you have experienced something of this nature? It's a common symptom of our world that we place the onus on another to abide by our 'rules' even if it doesn't feel right to them. We are guaranteed to fall, to fail, to betray, to make mis-takes in life because we are here to remember what it is to be divine. We can only receive what we give to ourselves. When we recognize the beauty of free will and understand that the universe always conspires on our behalf, we would never enroll anyone in our games, ever! We would understand the underlying meaning of what occurs around us as a barometer, showing us how to focus on what we choose so others can be free in their expression.

I apologized to my girlfriend in acknowledgement that I didn't honor my word and that I validated her feelings…and then I realized that I could no longer enter into these sorts of agreements again, unless I felt I could be my word. When the interaction arose with her ex, I didn't want to keep my word because I wanted to interfere – rightly or wrongly – because my intention was to honor her and in that moment I truly felt I could not just mind my own business. Now I know in my heart that I gained valuable insight into myself; I saw I was running a pattern of strongly wanting her love and approval, wanting to feel equal and to be included and loved and seen for my contribution. This upset was bound to happen because I was trying to please her and it wasn't my job to please her. I wasn't trusting that god was supplying exactly what she needed in order to be the best version of her.

The beauty of this whole scenario is that we did traverse it together in the moment and found the grace, until the mind took over and decided that rules needed to be put in place in order for her to love me. This too was also part of the perfect plan guiding each of us toward our next learning opportunity. Rejection is the re-direction toward a more focused intention. There was a condition she placed on loving herself and it's neither good nor bad, it simply is. Since the universe is new in every moment, there was a huge benefit for both of us to have had this interaction. We both can identify more clearly how to stay in love and generate from a place of faith, not fear. I got my lesson and I'm sure she received what was appropriate for her path and her self-realization, moving her closer toward her heart's desires. We are powerful intenders, focusers, and creators. We must stay mindful that a larger vision is being orchestrated to allow for self-realization on a broader scale.

How to communicate

Communication seems to be the number one cause of pain in relationships. It's either a lack of communication, an over-explanation, or the inability to articulate what you mean in a way that connects to another. My soul's purpose has been to deeply understand how to be an effective communicator, thereby receiving and achieving my desired goals. Communication has so many facets to it; there are layers upon layers of complications created along the way.

Here are 6 ways to be a more effective communicator in any relationship:

1. Listen.

One of the most powerful things anyone has ever said to me was: You will learn so much more if you just stop talking and hear what someone else has to say! Two ears, one mouth, use them in proportion.

I'm an over-communicator and quite verbose, and learning to listen has been a continual opportunity throughout my life. I often find myself wanting to interrupt, interject, defend, prove a point, clarify, instruct, share and express – and in all this glory, what ends up happening is that I don't listen. So ask yourself: Do I really listen when others speak? Do others have my undivided attention? Am I able to show up and be present and not be thinking about what I want to say next in order to be heard? And can I truly empty my mind and be in the flow of active listening?

Active listening is where you are willing to set everything aside and really participate with another, without an agenda or triggers. Easier said than done, I agree! It takes practice, practice and more practice. Being an active listener is still something I have to stay alert to when I'm caught up in my emotions. In fact, this is probably the time that we often check out; when we're only interested in the point we want to prove. It's not about being right or wrong or who wins the battle, because both lose out when the understanding breaks down.

When emotions are high we become stuck in the emotional body and all we can try for is that place of stability where suffering ceases. For some this is silence, for others it's resolve, or not wanting to stir up the emotions, for others it's a retreat into comfort and oblivion. Whatever your case or reason, it all boils down to this: we cannot effectively move forward in life when we are immersed in the drowning or droning of our own painful story.

How can you become an effective listener? Realize that life is either a projection or a reflection. We are either in the reflection of who we truly are and have adversity, judgment or fear about it. Or we are projecting our stuff, and playing our character defects (also known as 'opportunities') onto the other, insisting that what we're seeing is theirs!   Either way, it's all yours; it's all yours to reconcile within you, anyway you can.

2.   Take out a subscription for personal accountability!

Too many people subscribe to the victim mentality and this is where the water gets deep, because it implies that we are not at fault for our life, nor are we actively choosing to participate in it and create it. Ask yourself: What is it I am here to share? Check in to see if you're present with your moment of sharing, or if there's an underlying hidden agenda. Are you showing up to get something, to give something or to share something? And can you truly participate without wanting validation from another?

3.   Define what another is saying so that you can understand where they're coming from.

My father and I have been at odds my entire life, because we are so alike. He is a direct mirror of all the things that I strive to improve daily. Every time we see each other it's always very telling about where I am at with myself. Am I struggling? Am I pushing? Am I resisting? What is in my life? Am I needy? Do I have an agenda? Am I full of fear?

My father and I always respond to the underlying emotions that exist within each of us whenever we share time. My biggest fear is that if I am vulnerable or emotional, my father will not be able to support me or handle me. And so that is what I get every time – a father who cannot emotionally support me. Since I am such a huge believer that we are co-creating our life in order to learn and grow and move past our limitations, this is always the opportunity to see any latent fears I have about my relationship with life. My father is my number one trigger; he is the ultimate representation of the opposition I encounter within myself, because if I cannot handle who he is and I cannot accept things for what they are, then what am I doing?

The body has no recollection of time or space; it is only at the effect of each moment. But we can become more aware of the patterns that hold us in bondage and we can become alert to find a new feeling or way of dealing.

Sometimes I feel frustrated in the process, because I set intentions and in my own being I am joyfully expecting miracles, but I have found that if you're showing up to any relationship needing a person to fulfill you or make you feel better you may end up disappointed. If you can accept people where they are at all times, then when you express a need or desire and someone declines, you can find the joy in their refusal, and seek what you need elsewhere. There is no struggle, just a recognition that others can only give and share what is within each of us; we cannot force another to be what they are not, but we can encourage them to become the person they'd like to see in others.

4. Respond, not over-react!

I was told my whole life that I am an over-reactive person, that I wear my emotions on my sleeve and that I need to calm down! Well, when you're in the midst of a chakra blowout and you're an emotionally over-sensitive being, this doesn't help! The only remedy for this is to become master of your own energy and heighten your awareness to the motivating factor behind every outburst you encounter. All you experience is yourself, so it is impossible for another to speculate on how you should feel or react to any given circumstance. Your exploration and experience of how you view, see and feel the world is all so self-interpretative. Many people get caught up in the idea that if I can do it, so can you; if I can perceive something, then it must be true for you too.

I can say: "Don't lecture me", and you can react in a thousand different ways, depending on what comes up for you. You give the words life, meaning and energy; you are the one who determines what the words mean, based on what's in your memory banks. All interpretations are possible, from "I don't love you"; "You're not good enough"; "I'm not interested in you" and so on. When there's a reaction to a conversation, it's up to you to discover what the reaction means for you, with the understanding that there is always something beneath the surface – it's not just the words we're reacting to. The words take on a new meaning as a reflection of our own self worth and value. When you have understood this, and you can really identify your own feelings about what another has said, you will begin to concern yourself more with what it is they're really saying. How you interpret what they've said will either confirm your amazingness or your low self worth. And of course, understand that whatever you say will also be received by others, depending on how they feel about themselves. Remember: all you need is love. All we have in common is love. This is a universal language that everyone can enjoy without word or interpretations. Love is felt through touch, through a glance, through a smile. When we remember this, the world becomes united under a common bond – the unspoken communication of understanding, the desire to see everyone feel good.

5. Be clear.

But what does that really mean? Being clear is about identifying what it is you are wanting the other person to receive from your communication. Is there a double meaning in what you're saying? Are you being evasive? Do you twist the words to meet your needs? Are you coercive in order to get what you want? Are you seeking love and approval when you are speaking? Are you fixated on what you can't change and what's already transpired? Focus on what you'd love to see occur, unwavering, the people you communicate with will either tire out because you no longer react, will meet you in your vision, or will step away to harness what they need in their own timing. No matter what, it's up to you to clearly know the life you choose to lead. Focus, focus, focus. This is your gateway to expanding and dropping into the field of possibility where the past has no bearing on the future since the universe is new in every moment to create with.

6. Find a common goal.

In order for a relationship to work, there must be a common denominator, a shared vision for the future. When we can connect to our inspiration of what it is we are choosing to share, we can move by Divine will into our inspired action. When this is shared with loved ones, that inspired action becomes a tangible force, more easily manifested. You will know in the unfoldment of a relationship if you see eye to eye over time, or if your sharing works to expand your viewpoints. Whatever the way, you are always being given opportunities to celebrate what you are experiencing and find the benefits of every interaction. Every person, place or situation you may encounter on your path will deliver to you insights into the person you choose to be. We are stacking life's experiences in order to have a more refined focus in experiencing what works and what doesn't work, that life is the moment of circumstance at hand. How you handle yourself every time you come in contact with the same pattern will determine where you go next. If there is still gain in the pain then that is a common goal to traverse through too. The common goal isn't to always agree, the common goal is to align with what will meet your greater needs for the full experience of the life you seek. Life is to be shared and when we find a meeting of the minds, and a meeting of hearts in a united position, we thrive and prosper our humanity. What you do for you, you do for all of humanity. Personal development is the key to an ever-expanding universe of what you enjoy perceiving.

You give the story meaning and you decide to either find the path that will make way for your dreams or you go against the current so many times that you blame and drown in your own concept of a limited reality. The common goal is to agree to disagree and honor the path that each individual seeks. If it is for you, it will come toward you; when it no longer aligns, the universe will find a new path or direction for you to traverse. Stay open; accepting the unacceptable now makes room for possibility and truth to come into play. The key to life is play, play with your options, play out all scenarios, and envision your goals being realized. The people who play on the other side will stay as long as the game serves their purpose to realize their personal vision for life. You will always find participants on the path that will match you where you are. As you progress they will either join you or new ones will appear to gain deeper insight into what you are refining, reframing, refreshing, regaining and resetting.

How do we cope with people who will not listen?

To be listened to, first you must practice the art of listening. I find that this is often the biggest struggle in relationships, because people expect not to be heard and so they don't bother to speak and vice versa – people who expect to be heard may not be good listeners. Become masterful at listening to yourself first. Self-knowledge produces self-mastery.

Ask yourself: Do I really hear people when they speak? Am I a good listener? I grew up in a family where no one listened. In fact it was one interruption upon another. None of us listened and in order to be heard, we would shout, thinking that if we spoke loud enough, we would be heard! But all it really did was create a yelling match and no one heard anything; instead, we all strained our voices and trashed our nervous systems.

So listening became a huge issue in my life, and I still have to be very cognizant of listening to this day, as I have a tendency to interrupt people because I become impatient and eager, and think that what I'm saying is more relevant. I have to practice active listening daily, and really bring my attention to it when someone is speaking. Every day I become a better listener. Give yourself one day a week where you will practice listening; notice throughout that day when you realize you're not listening; notice how many times you interrupt people mid-sentence; and notice if you're the type of person who asks a lot of questions but doesn't wait for the reply. These are all things to be aware of for those of you who don't have a natural tendency to listen.

And for those who are already amazing listeners, and who interact with us poor listeners – encourage us to be aware of opportunities to be better participants. Listening is an active role! The way to make people feel valued and important is to really give them your undivided attention and listen. When people feel heard, they'll want to share more time with you, because they'll feel safe and they'll feel like you really care. In fact this is an excellent demonstration of caring for another and what they have to share.

There are three parts to listening:

1. Listen to yourself.

Get to know you. We often make others responsible when we are not heard, but what's really occurring is that we don't listen to ourselves first. Therefore we attract others who appear to be poor listeners – just like us! If you have this mantra: no one ever listens to me, I guarantee that is the experience you will continually call into your life. People will listen to you, but you won't be able to see it.

What if you flipped the script and you now believed: "Everyone listens to me. I am always heard and appreciated for what I share"? The feedback would be completely different. You would expect and experience everyone listening to you.

Go within see what you believe about listening.

2. Be an outstanding listener in your conversations with others.

Try this mantra: "I am an amazing listener, people love to share with me, they feel heard and acknowledged."

3. When listening, be aware of the breath to keep you in the moment of presence.

Listening is about being present, so you can respond authentically in the moment. It's like a game of tennis – you know the ball is coming your way, so you keep yourself open, positioning yourself where you need to be on every pass. Listening is interactive – be an active listener.

Power, not force

We cannot demand an audience; life is not for us to push for what we want, it's for us to receive what we choose. If you're wanting to give a presentation and the content you are sharing has no importance to anyone because it's self-edifying, you may not command an audience to listen…force never yields the desired results, it only yields confrontation and adversity. However, if you want to share in life and you want an audience, then people will willingly and happily appear to you. You do not have to coerce them into it. Demanding what you want never seems as satisfying when you receive it, because it comes through duress. Asking for what you want and allowing someone the option of giving it, supports you in your understanding of value and worthiness – when another shares, they do so from choice and not obligation, so both of you can enjoy the exchange more fully.

We cannot force another to stop on the spot what they are doing. They choose to either go along with your request or not and if you demand someone stop speaking and they continue, what do you do next? If you find it uncomfortable either move your person or move your position of thinking! If you cannot do either and the force is to fight, then play that out too – you will only gain valuable insight from the interplay. The mere fact that there is force on one end may lead to opposition on the other end. Until it dispels itself, that force will continue to rear its head. When you learn to respond in a new way and you see the situation for what it is – two individuals who want to feel heard, loved, appreciated and honored – then the small self softens and the power play of duress ceases. The common denominator is to love and understand the wisdom in what's occurring.

The power behind force is that it quickens the recognition of what underlies each individual's position. You'll either merge into agreements or you'll move on to experience another version of this. Force is the fast track to refinement! Once the dusts settles, you can be certain to find valuable pearls from your interactions, clearly illuminating to you the depth of what was underlying the force to begin with.

Most people lack the courage to ask for what they want, because they often don't know what they want. The courage to ask comes when you can identify what you want. I encounter this dilemma with so many of my clients; they are afraid to tell the truth or to ask for what they need. So they suppress their wants and desires and they expect others to be mind readers. They become victim to entitlement and they think the world owes them something. So resentment builds up, and they start complaining. Passive-aggressive tendencies emerge because they're so afraid to tell people what they really think and how they feel for fear of discomfort, pain, or being abandoned or abused. They silently suffer and use passive-aggressive victim-perpetrator devices in order to staunch the pain they feel inside. Everyone knows deep inside what it is they truly feel, but the veils of illusion, the lack of appreciation and the ego stand in the way of us truly for-giving our fellow man and opening to supporting people in their pain, wherever they are at.

Can we say what we mean and mean what we say? Is life giving you what you give it? If you're unable to identify what it is you are feeling, how can you articulate your needs? If we were to forge agreements with others before we laid into them with guilt, anger and fear, we may actually achieve harmonious communication. But the willingness of the participants is key; you cannot force someone to change or listen. I've found in my own experiences when I have so desperately wanted to be heard that these were the times I met with most resistance. I was so attached to proving my point or sounding intelligent or satisfying my ego that I would try to force people into listening, by speaking loudly or insistently, and I would not back down until my point had been made. I found it very challenging to sit passively or quietly by when I was desperate to defend myself, and my need to fight to the death was more important than my need to be understood.

If there are people in your life who will not listen to you, you cannot force them to make them choose your way; it will only hinder your progress, so there has to be an agreement made within the self to resolve to agree to disagree. Agree to allow others their various styles of communication. Agree to explore and ask what you can do to be a better participant in your relationships. Agree to understand. Agree to find a blessing in whatever it is that is being withheld. Agree to see it as a signpost for your next destination. Agree to stand in your truth, expressed or unexpressed.

I cannot force anyone to change. But what I can do is observe the very thing that is presenting itself as an annoyance or inconvenience for me, and resolve it in myself. If there is something in you do that I do not approve of, I can either participate or not participate. If I choose to participate and you have made it clear that you won't stop doing what you're doing, then I have to find a new way to handle my reactions. Or I can choose to lovingly walk away in integrity of my truth; which is, I will not tolerate this behavior in you because it brings up too much in me that I am unwilling to address at this time, because I don't know how to manage my emotions. What you may discover is that the very thing you run from is the very thing that follows you from relationship to relationship. The resolution occurs when you are willing to heal that pattern within yourself; you stop blaming every person who evokes it, instead recognizing the deep strand within you that needs stretching in order to develop and grow. The person with whom you experienced that reaction may change but the pattern remains the same.

How do we continue our evolution of growth when the people around us cannot move past their own limitations and triggers? People are signposts on the path...leading you to your next destination.

1. Give permission for them to grow. That's the most loving way to actualize their potential.

2. Understand all sides...step into the other's shoes, and understand that we are all interacting with one another's patterns.

3. Personal accountability. When you take accountability for the life you live, you then have the opportunity to make

new choices that supports what it is you are truly desiring.

4. Possess nothing, enjoy everything. Possessiveness of life is the poison that obliterates our freedom. Every possession you acquire is temporary, but every feeling you awaken is yours for eternity. This life is to be enjoyed, others are to be celebrated, but in the desire to own and possess the world around us, we become attached and angry because we can never possess another. We can only invest in and choose to participate. Even our life mates are not our property; they are a unique entity capable of formulating their own ideas.

5. We come together to understand ourselves. You are only talking to yourself to remind yourself of what it is you want to be, so listen to your own advice – it's probably better advice than you can receive from others, because it comes from you own personal filter. The advice you seek is the advice you'll usually give. Every interaction I have helps me to better understand who I am through the reflection of another's behaviors.

6. Heal the other, by healing yourself.

Is honesty the best policy?

I often work with people whose number one complaint is that they want honest relationships; they want people in their lives to have the courage to tell the truth. Unfortunately this is probably one of the most challenging aspects of any relationship. Is honesty the best policy, and are omissions considered lying? When a client tells me they're infuriated because someone has lied to them, or omitted information, I ask them to ask themselves: where have you been lying to yourself, or omitting information in your relations with others? This provokes and incites them to look within and really ask: do I speak my truth, am I an honest person? I've found that we will only attract an experience we do not prefer because it allows us to see something within ourselves that we need to heal. Only in the revelation of what is in need of healing will change come.

I visited a client who contracted bronchitis, accompanied by a cough and a terrible sore throat. We discovered that she was having a moral dilemma regarding the agreement she had made with her boyfriend, who was 3,000 miles away, and who she only saw every four months or so. They agreed to be monogamous, which was not really an agreement that resonated for her. She was discovering in herself that she was a very affectionate, free, open-minded curious type who loved to love, so being alone at 17 without her current partner became a problem for her; she was torn between being happy with where she was at, and wanting to be where she was not. She had agreed with her partner that they would stay loyal and faithful while they were apart, but as time went on and the days grew longer she realized she was in need of companionship and physical love. She was emotionally loyal, but she wanted to experience the essence of her flesh, and the joy of sharing and caring, and the excitement of new people and situations, just for the experience of it. This was not her agreement with her boyfriend, so what she started experiencing was a deep inner struggle of in-congruency. Her inner truth said, be free, be in love, experience life and when you encounter the next phase, you will be emotionally present to what is there. But in the meantime live, learn, grow…

So she started lying. But we are all connected and linked, especially to the ones we share a conscious, energetic, active bond with. And so the boyfriend began to call, saying, "You don't love me, tell me who he is," and she would lie and deny there was anything going on. Little by little the lies shut down her immune system and she created all these symptoms in order to not deal with what was happening. She went into guilt, embarrassment and sadness. The need for attention and love was so present that she literally had to create an extreme case of acute asthmatic bronchitis; she could not bear the pain in her heart that it left her short of breath. When I showed up, we examined what was happening, without any moral judgment as to right or wrong. We looked at her belief system, what she was saying, who she was being and what message she wanted to convey to the world. She was involved with another man – all very innocent – but the boyfriend was intuitive and right, and she was being dishonest. She did love her boyfriend and so her heart was loyal but she recognized that, had there been no distance between them, there would be no reason to seek love and affection elsewhere. She admitted that she was lonely and curious. When she understood that all she had to do was be honest to what was true for her, her symptoms started to melt away one by one. She realized she was in an agreement that did not suit her needs, and that in order to move forward and feel good, she would need to continue being aware of what was comfortable for her and have the courage to be who she really was, and not fit in because she was afraid of loss and rejection.

Inevitably, if she was unable to see what she was unconsciously creating, she may very well have created the loss that she feared. Now that her eyes were open to the truth she could make new choices for her future. Her illness was an opportunity to uncover the moral struggle and come up with a solution that sat well with the person she discovered herself to be. The truth really does set you free and even if it's only the discovery within yourself, this alone will heal the pain we create for ourselves. So this girl's lesson was that, in order to feel good, she would have to speak her truth, ask for what suits the situation and allow herself to receive the highest best outcome for all involved. Florence Scovel Shinn always says you cannot lose what is yours, so in this case, if this is the man for her, these discoveries will now set the foundation for a strong relationship together, one that may be able to stand the test of time.

How can you learn to loosen the grip and not fear losing what is precious to you?

In the above case, loosening her grip on the relationship is the only choice this girl can make. If she didn't, she would have to compromise her own values and desires to make sure that the man stayed in her life. When we make space for another to experience themselves and the world around them, we are also making space for ourselves to do the same. If you cannot lose what is yours, then loosening the grip will only create the way to know that what you're sharing with another is true. Through your co-creative powers, spirit will deliver the right people, places and situations in order to make that which serves your highest good appear.

I decided that my relationship with my own partner was an honor, not an obligation, and that if he was to be the one for me, I needed to make allowances for our individual growth processes. In the past I held on so tight that every man I ever loved left me, because that's what I feared the most. In addition, I was conditioned to believe that in order to keep love in your life, you had to earn it, and if you didn't demonstrate value and worthiness, you would be left alone. So I continuously recreated my story, my by-line, in every relationship I had until my most current relationship, where I awoke to the fact that you cannot force someone to be with you. You can only be the best person you know how to be and allow for the reflections and lessons to emerge. I do not want to own another's soul; I want to have the honor to participate with another through choice. It is not always easy, reflecting the parts of ourselves that demonstrate our humanity, but it is through humanity that we can find the strength to continue on the journey. When you know that every person who comes upon your path is there to show you who you are, then you will make space for these comings and goings in your life, because you will always strive toward self-realization and self-love. I do not believe that you can lose a person, or that anyone can abandon me anymore. What I've discovered is that I used to create the appearance of abandonment in my outer circumstances, because abandonment has always been me with me. I use to abandon myself because of my belief system, my idea that love is full of pain and longing.

I've had to rewrite my script and play a new tune, in order to create a looser grip on life, on a more loving, allowing, accepting, and surrendered path. My new creed is: Love is here for me now. Love is joyful and fun. In the past, I chose to believe that I was not loveable and that no matter what I did or how I behaved, I would never be good enough. I also focused on so many of the things I detested in my partner, that ultimately every transgression of pain was bestowed upon, me because I believed in self-punishment. In fact, self-punishment was a language that comforted my soul. Pain, lack, loss, hurt, and victimhood were all there. Loosening the grip was just a theory; I couldn't loosen the grip to anything in my life because that would mean I would lose, and that would confirm my story that I sucked. Because I didn't loosen the grip and allow my partners their exploration, curiosity, judgment and experiences, one by one they left, saying, "Nothing is ever good enough for you; all you do is complain and what's fun about that?" They were right, I always looked for what was wrong and I always found a way to not celebrate them, but made them into the problem. Instead of humbly looking at myself, I would blame them. I was the problem, my belief system was the problem, and I constantly was creating what I did not want through my actions, words and deeds.

But I came to learn that it's never about the other person, it is 100% about you. If you can awaken to this understanding, then the journey becomes a beautiful exploration of discovering who you really are, and remembering the divinity of each and every soul you encounter along the way as a gift to remind you of your humanity and Divinity united. Loosening the grip implies making space for another to be expressed and finding the honor in that participation. Loosening the grip implies, seek within what it is you are attaching yourself to. Loosening the grip implies allowing people to become the outer barometer of what it is that is going on inside of you – the reflection of the inner work you need to do within yourself. Loosening the grip implies letting go of what you think life needs to be, and making room for what you'd really like to see.

Possess nothing, enjoy everything.

This is a prime example of how we think we possess one another. We preface everything as mine – my boyfriend, my book, my home, etc. The reality is we can never truly own anything. However, we can enjoy everything. Possessiveness is where pain is created, because we get caught in the illusion that someone owes us something, and there has to be a direct balance in life. That when we give, we must receive. We are all caught in the illusion that the giving isn't the receiving; when we give we receive the act of giving freely. We think that what we have is ours. We have lost the honor of participating with our things and people, and have accorded deep meaning to our possessions – we have even given our power away to them, as a way of measuring our worthiness. We have lost ourselves in the material world. Our possessions are just a reflection of everything that is before us – a signature of energy that combines itself with our association to that object or person.

We have deeply rooted ourselves in feeling good about ourselves through our acquaintances, homes, partners, clothes, cars – many people today are defined by what they know and what they have. But in doing so, we have lost the essence of what really matters, which is that all that we possess or see outside of us is a reflection of what we feel within ourselves. We have generated these depictions and representations through the material world so that we can see who we truly are, and see the beauty that lies within. Beauty is in the eye of the beholder and whatever is reflecting outside of you, wherever you seek your solace, with whomever you seek your soul satisfaction, each and every one of these relationships are aspects of you. But I have seen all too often that even in these beautiful reminders of what we are, that we are not enjoying our possessions, but have become slaves to them. They have possessed us. I have met many people who possess beauty and power but who have lost sight of why they wanted it in the first place. They no longer enjoy what they possess; in fact their possessions have become burdensome, or the reason they decided to attain all this wealth to begin with has become a distant memory. All they do is seek the next thing in order to feel the fulfillment they once had.

I once worked with a very famous man who simply had it all – fame, glory, money, talent looks, family, everything. The world loved this man, but he was one of the loneliest people I had ever met. He clearly was able to attain possessions but what he truly sought to possess was the ability to enjoy it all. So he began seeking through self-introspection, taking risky journeys across the land, lifting the veil of illusion to discover the reason he needed to possess so much was in order to find self-love. He just needed a larger demonstration than most, to really understand how beloved he was. The fame and the possessions were to teach and remind him that without love for one's self, that all he possessed meant nothing. He could continue doing movie after movie, buying one fun toy after another, moving from relationship to relationship, but he could never possess anything, as it was all a temporary solution to a larger dilemma. What he sought was love, true love, love that knows no borders, nor time nor space. He was seeking love and approval from himself; seeking to reunite with the infinite Divine mind within all things and from which all things are fashioned from. He was seeking self-realization, merging his humanity and divinity to understand his spiritual assignment and purpose. He ultimately found it through the shedding and letting go of the false identity that had many possessions; he found it through the reflection of god's greatest gift, that of love. He saw himself through the eyes of love. He saw that he was not amazing because he amassed fame and fortune. He was amazing because of his ability to express his fame and fortune, and in doing so, teach self-love. He could do this, because he learned the true meaning of life – to love thyself and the world will be given to you.

What does this mean to enjoy what you seemingly possess instead of possessing what you enjoy? I have a client who was had been married for 17 years, but she had decided to abandon the relationship 8 years into it, because she was not enjoying what she possessed. She became very detached from the honor of this sharing, which led to jealousy, a sense of entitlement, resentment, anger, hurt, pain and discord. She withheld her love from her partner, thereby withholding it from herself. She sought refuge in relationships with others due to her inability to access the love, nurturing and tenderness available from her partner. She disassociated herself from her life and her true essence and became a master of living in duality. All the while she was yearning for freedom, she became a passive-aggressive person in her expressions, due to the fact that she needed constant love, approval, adoration and servitude in order to feel alive. She lied to herself and her family in order to hide from the pain she felt inside; she judged herself for her incongruent actions, yet couldn't stop the painful cycle. She ran from herself and the life she created because she was constantly dueling with what her head said and what her heart wanted. Her relationships all devolved into possessiveness for fear of loss; her identity was wrapped up in the illusion of her titles and obligations, rather than in her be-ingress and self-realizations.

Throughout the course of our work, I was able to help this client see that everything she ever created was a co-creation with the Creator and that the life she was living was a by-product of ingrained patterns from her childhood, where she believed she was not worthy of receiving love and being celebrated for her playful, joyous nature. She learned that the only way to have love was to get it through subtle manipulation, misuse of sexuality and the illusion of guilt and obligation.

Unspoken communication

Everything we do and say has an impact upon the planet. We are not an isolated entity unto ourselves; we are sharing in an integrated whole where everything you do for yourself affects that world. We are united under the planetary solar system and nothing would exist if not for the rising sun and evening moonshine. We are cycles and seasons, all at the effect of our universal consciousness under the influence of Divine intervention. We also have the beauty of free will, combined with destiny's path and the intention of the highest good in order to learn create and grow.

What we are saying is just as important as what we aren't saying; it is all a communication that leads to the unraveling of our path. To have strength and be powerful, we must become aware of the unspoken dialogue we have with ourselves and the creative force within that is helping to navigate our path. Each and every one of us was born with a purpose on this planet, and it is up to all of us to discover what that is and what inspires our passion for living. Once we understand that we are all generators of information and that we are always outputting messages and signals, then we can start to purposefully direct this output.

What you say and do speaks volumes...become aware of the message you are conveying and take personal responsibility for what that creates in and around you.

Can we manifest our fears?

Absolutely, however this is nothing to fear. Our fears represent the F.orgetting E.very A.wesome R.eality in which we live... so a fear realized shows us the opposite of what it was we were truly wanting to create.

There is a pattern within me that has shown up for years concerning my father, that no matter how many times I thought I had graduated to the other side, spirit would continually provide me with new people and situations in which to address these fears, from many different perspectives and angles. Just when I thought, "Whew, it's complete, it won't repeat," the next wave of fear would occur, and the lesson always came stronger and more impactful. What I discovered however, that little by little as you keep chipping away at your sculpture, ultimately what will remain is the masterpiece – like Michelangelo's David. But it is a gradual process of self-discovery that can take years and it requires patience and the ability to see the end in sight. You must know the destination of your descent and stay steady on course, and when the obstacles present themselves, slow down and do whatever it takes to get over the hurdles and continue forging ahead, knowing that you will arrive when you are supposed to.

I have often struggled with remaining faithful to this journey as I have seen the end in sight. I know my direction, but at times it can seem like I am so off the path that there is no way I will ever arrive at my desired goal. But what I continuously discover is that every stop along the way is my opportunity to grow, and through this expedition I only become stronger for the next encounter. I've set clear intentions that my path comes for the highest good. When I am unwavering in my belief that the universe responds to my call, and I have made myself aware of the obstacles that could impede my path, I become more and more prepared to handle these hurdles more gracefully. One of my biggest patterns in life that I have had to overcome is letting go of people…and the idea that when someone does not choose to include you, that this perceived rejection is really your protection. We draw to ourselves what will grow us into our best self. This may not always appear in the way you think, as we sometimes attach ourselves to things and then we discover later that it was more magnificent than we could ever conjure in our own mind. This is the majesty of divinity working alongside to make way for what is your greatest life path.

I have created situations where I have come to understand that I will never be without, as long as I remember that everything I attain, attract, or reflect comes from within my own context of how I feel about me. My outer reality will always show up supporting and demonstrating to me what it is I am truly feeling and needing to discover. I have claimed to live a life of integrity and truth, and so this is what is upon me – I teach what I preach. To truly understand this, you must deeply, intimately experience the ins and outs of how it all works.

When fear gets in the way

Often times fear is the gateway for fast growth, because in order to reach what our hearts and minds desire, we may need to recognize what is preventing us from truly and richly experiencing our joy.

When I pray and ask for the highest good, I am often surprised when very unexpected and seemingly painful experiences arise. But when I look back I can see how the Divine was intervening in ways that were non-conventional in order for me to reach the desired outcome for a more truthful, peaceful, harmonious path.

Fear is a catalyst for growth, for us to move from humanity into divinity. Find Every Awesome Reality (F.E.A.R.) is a pathway to a new understanding of that which stands between what you have and what you want. Fear can direct you exactly into that perfect place of surrender, where you will benefit from its presence it's a calling to pay attention. How we have defined fear culturally is that it is the threatened ego that one might loose or lack something as opposed to gain in perception and opportunity?

I am such a powerful Creator that when I experience a strong fear I will usually get the opportunity to see it expressed immediately. This is how I have grown so quickly, because in the end I see that what I fear is never as bad as I had anticipated – and if what is undesired comes to pass, then so what…

Something new always comes from experiencing the fear, something that makes way for me to become still, set the restart button, and ask myself: what do I really want next and what have I learned from this experience? And in order to create something new, what will I need to do to support my **F**.inding **E**.very **A**.wesome **R**.eality as opposed to **F**.orgetting **E**.very **A**.wesome **R**.eality?

So embrace what troubles you and when the fear becomes so overpowering that you can no longer avoid it, surrender into it, let it play itself out if need be, and then make intentional choices to align yourself with what it is you truly want and how it is you really want to feel. There is never a wrong way, there is only finding a way.

The Divine provides new things for me to experience so I can understand what it feels to walk a mile in someone else's shoes. I often use the example of the garbage dumpster: Imagine you're in a foreign county, and you're walking down a narrow alley way and you see a garbage dumpster with unintelligible writing on it. You comment to your friend, "Wow, how cool is this dumpster with its strange lettering," because you've found the beauty in this new moment; you've never seen this place before or this object.

One day I gave this example to a client, and I was inviting him to apply this method to his daily life: Imagine your life here as if you're on permanent vacation. Everywhere you go you find the beauty and magic of everything you find, especially those things that we have the most judgment on, like our trash. You don't have to escape your everyday life to have fun; your every-day surroundings could invoke more magic than you know, you just have to be willing to see what is really before you and stay in a neutral place of observance and celebration.

My client was grateful and said he would start to apply this vacation concept in his everyday life, to see if he could discover the awe in where he was right now. He would take the time to really look around and be thankful for all that he participated in, including people, places and situations.

The very next day I went to check my mail and that of my neighbor who was out of town. There were some flyers that I didn't want so I went to the dumpster, opened it up and dropped them in. When I got upstairs I realized I had dropped the key to my neighbor's apartment somewhere along the way. I retraced my footsteps; there was nothing on the path. It dawned on me that I had dropped the key in the dumpster! I changed my clothes and started to dig around in the dumpster...and I had to laugh, thinking about what I had told my client the day before, about seeing the beauty in the dumpster! Lo and behold, I was being presented with a new opportunity to not only celebrate the container of trash, but to get down and dirty into the trash itself.

I had always wondered what it felt to be homeless and obliged to dig in the trash, and there I was, getting my own personal experience – to walk a mile in the shoes of many. I wasn't sure how easy it would be to find the key, but I was willing to try. So I lifted the lid and started pulling out various pieces of trash, one by one. Flies were swarming and it all stank of rotting food. It was a very warm day and there I was in an alleyway on July 4, picking through the trash! Ironically, I had been scheduled to fly out to the Virgin Islands the day before, for a beautiful work vacation, but the trip had been cancelled, making it harder to find any appreciation for this experience.

I spotted a young boy coming down the alley so I asked if he would help me lift the trash onto its side, which he did before meandering off. There were some kids and a man in the alleyway looking on; the man came over with a stick and he offered to help. He suggested turning the dumpster over, so we could see better. I found some plastic bags in my apartment, to protect my hands, and I suddenly realized how the universe was supporting me in this seemingly trashy moment. The young and handsome man was a professional boxer, so he was big and strong and he lifted that dumpster like He-Man! I was actually having fun now, chatting away with this cute French boxer! A few moments before, I was feeling a little bummed about being alone and at home, and here was Divine intervention. We cleared all the trash and I had just about given up, but there, under a leaf, my French companion found the key! I was so excited I was jumping up and down for joy – I hugged this perfect stranger for helping me find the key. I felt so loved and supported, and I had experienced something I never would have volunteered to do in this lifetime: I developed a deep sympathy and compassion for the homeless and I felt like I had a deeper understanding of the humility of a person who chooses a life in the trash. I made a new friend, I felt oneness and I shared love. I was ecstatic, overjoyed and I felt so blessed. So it goes to show that we teach what we learn, and life sometimes will give you a more intimate, deeper way to understand the world in a way you could have never conjured yourself. That is the magic of allowing, letting go and F.inding E.very A.wesome R.eality… You get to see that nothing is ever as bad as it seems and that it is always your attitude that creates your interpretation of life.

Fear is the number one thing that prevents us from going for what we want: Fear of not being loved, fear of failure, fear of loneliness, fear of rejection. I was afraid to write this book for many years, as I feared that what I have to say would be of no importance to anyone. But the only way to overcome fear is to face it head on. So here you have it – I'm writing to you because I have a message to share from my experience of life…and if you are reading this book, then it goes to show that all my experiences have served me well, as I am facing what I fear now with you. You may love what you read and you may not, but I commend you for keeping an open mind and seeking solutions to improve your life, to learn how to live in love more consistently with more ease.

Forget everything and remember

In forgetting everything, we make way for remembering what it is we are all here to do – and that is love. We are here to remember the essence of our being; we are here to remember to play; we are here to vibrate and energize one another; we are here to learn. Fear is our opportunity to encounter our excitement. I've come to realize that whatever I fear can only come to pass – and then when and if it does, it gives me the opportunity to approach it differently and change the pattern within me. As I turned 35, life was smooth – in fact I was living life the way I always saw myself doing. I was social, happy, lively and vibrant, making love, working, prospering, learning and growing, exercising and eating impeccably – in fact it was so uplifting I was just delirious with the excitement of every new day. I felt purposeful, fulfilled and alive;

I felt like I was attaining my goals. I felt included, loved and valued, and I was living from my essence. But as the week of my 35th birthday drew near, I became so afraid that the new friendships I had forged would disappear; that the love and freedom and openness would go away; that the money would dry up and that the old me would be discovered. It felt like maybe I wasn't really this strong, empowered channel of love and truth – that I was a farce. How could it last? Did I deserve all this? Surely something would go wrong and prove that nothing this good can last. Up until then, I'd never had it so smooth. I felt I was living life to the fullest, and the universe was loving me so fully, deeply and richly that I just couldn't maintain it. I was waiting for the other shoe to drop, because this was my pattern: up and down and round and round. This was what I had been teaching: how to weather the storm and come out stronger than before.

Now this time around I saw it coming, but it was almost like a snowball effect – I couldn't get out of the way, I was bound to be gathered up and run over. The fear intensified so much that on my birthday I revisited deeply entrenched patterns. I was mystified, deeply disappointed and in shock. How could I be so off course, disillusioned and participating in this painful exchange, with all my training, awareness and experience? Someone of my ability should not be revisiting the past to this magnitude. Then I saw the perfection of it all – the Divine mind working in all things to collaborate with each and every little encounter to bring me to this point. I stood looking at myself saying, "Wow, I never thought I'd be this person at 35, but in fact I love who I've become. I love what I've done to achieve this deep sense of inner knowing, empowerment and awareness." I felt proud of my willingness to be so committed to my awakening, but let me tell you, it didn't come as I had thought it would. I had seen myself at 35: married, living in a huge house on the water, famous and at the top of my game in all areas of my life. In order to have this, I had to have every single experience along the way and I truly felt that what I was seeking and longing for was not far from my path. In fact it felt the closest I've ever experienced, and all I could say was, "Thank you for the learning, I'm ready for greatness, I'm ready for my Divine life mate, I'm ready for my fame and fortune." But of course I wasn't really…fear took over and spirit still had some deep lessons in store for me.

I committed myself to being a person who walks their talk, but in order to achieve this I still had some hurdles to overcome and that was my deepest, darkest fear. Am I really there yet? Am I good enough? Is it really happening? Can I really have done enough work to now live in the glory and play of all I've amassed spiritually, mentally and physically? Am I ready to lead?

I was so afraid of my power that once again I needed to revisit insecurity, shriveling up, giving away my light in order to be loved. I questioned why we even try if we're just destined to fail…what's the point? Where's my reward? How come I have to lose everything again? I'm really happy, I love what I am and who's around me, and what I'm teaching and creating…

Well, spirit always has my highest interest in mind, and these lessons came in such a way that it would either catapult me into my greatness or I would die trying. Happily enough, I am better than ever now; I overcame my biggest fear by identifying the core issue that had been my pattern my whole life, in every relationship and in every area of my life. Determined to overcome and become my greatness, I started to heal the pattern within. I was sent to a woman friend who was able to help me in the way I had helped so many. I had prayed for her; I had prayed that god would give me someone who did my work, and who could help me shift at lightning speed by illuminating to me what it was I was not seeing, and help me draw out the theme that echoed in every area of my life. I realized in that moment once again what a powerful manifestor I was; not only did I manifest my fears, but I did so in such a way that I had nothing to lose. All I could do was surrender, pray, say 'thank you', align my energies with what I know I wanted to create, and identify how this pattern was preventing me from entering the new phase of my life. If I was able to overcome this, I truly would have graduated to the next level and could live the life I always knew was for me. I would know that the tools I was teaching worked beautifully, and that when I let go and allowed for my lessons to come, they showed up perfectly. I gracefully stepped through and did it differently than ever before.

When I align and allow for Divine timing, and when I stay in love willingly, to see and serve, I find the hidden blessings in all that there is. By listening to my intuition, and trusting that spirit will deliver all the right people, places and situations to grow me into my best self, well then it seems to me that life becomes a moment-to-moment creation of releasing, surrendering, accepting, allowing, and embracing. All I have to do is be willing to feel, deal and allow the path to reveal what is in accordance with Divine will, and then play…. enjoy the glory of the grace and ease, and let opportunity be all I can see.

Affirmations for empowerment

☐ I ask to be received with an open heart and an open mind and that I receive with an open heart and open mind for the highest good of all.

☐ I ask to be guided to the right people, places and situations that will grow me into my highest self.

☐ I send the light ahead and ask that all events be Divinely orchestrated to support me living and fulfilling my passions.

☐ I take inspired action toward those things that bring me joy, inspiration, awareness and upliftment. I let go and go with the flow. I Love living Openly, Vibrantly, Energetically in every moment. I always have a choice. Life is an honor. I am grateful for all my possessions, for the people in my life and for the opportunities to grow. I am an amazing communicator. I let people be who they are, and I celebrate people in their humanity. I trust that I am always being delivered the highest light teachings. I am for-sharing and for-giving.

☐ Today I am an instrument of inspired action, fulfilling the Divine plan from the Divine mind that creates all existence! I make demonstrations of my faith in every action I take! My demonstrations reap fulfillment in all areas of my life.

☐ God, please bring me people, places and situations that bring me in alignment with my purpose here on earth, that I may be guided to that which fulfills the highest plan for us all. Use me as an instrument of your grace and glory, as a messenger of love, reminding and revealing the truth to humanity. Love is all there is!

Change the station

If you don't like the station – change it. You always have a choice, be empowered by the choices you make…they are always correct for your learning curve!

Love deeply, look clearly, laugh loudly, dance freely, love openly, live joyously, feel everything, grow upward, strengthen your weaknesses, learn something new every step of the way, focus on service, serve your focus, melt, shine, breathe, sense, taste, touch, feel, engage the senses, take pleasure in your choices, make lots of love, greet the day in love, smile, share, be present – that is the gift of grace. Take your time, eat slowly, express, speak your truth, believe in the dream, see the beauty within, touch and hug someone daily, connect to the light, embrace the shadow, accept the differences, celebrate everyone, remember you are perfection, don't change, become and remember who you were born to be, love yourself, love, love, love, love…

Every person leads you to your next thing. We are all blessings to each other on the path and all is a representation of where we want to arrive at or even where we currently are.

Affirmations for a partner

- ☐ I let go and let god guide me to my Divine partner with ease.

- ☐ Thank you god for guiding me to my Divine partner with ease.

"Circumstances don't matter; only state of being matters. What state of being do I prefer?" -Bashar.

CHAPTER SIX SUMMARY: RELATIONSHIPS

There is a time and place for all things and that is why the model of BEING is to be present to what is right now.

Give a little time and space before making rash decisions, time can serve as an amazing buffer to having clarity and acting from an empowered place of choice and self knowing.

No one can treat you poorly because the standard of how you are treated is determined by how you treat yourself. No one else is to blame.

Stepping away does not denote giving up. Follow your heart. In the avoidance of what you don't want and by adhering to the rules of others, you will never win. However if you honor what appears in the name of love then choices can be made from a place of peace and stillness.

Can you see past the limitations of others and see their perfection, their potential realized, and that they are exactly as they need to be in their perfect place? When we experience withdrawal, rejection or cruelty, we have to know that we are in charge of how we perceive it and we turn the story in our favor and find the blessing, or we find another excuse to substantiate some illusion we have told ourselves. There is perfection in both sides as long as you remember that it's not what is occurring that's upsetting you. It's your thoughts about what you're experiencing that is upsetting you!

If you look for what's wrong you'll find it. If you think you've done something wrong then you will find that too. There is no wrong, there is only choice. If I can't please you or my behavior offends you then you have a choice how to respond. You could blow it off, you could laugh it off, you could personalize it as a personal affront to you, you could say I don't relate with people who do x, y, z behaviors and then you have your laundry list. I guarantee if that's what you want to avoid that's what you'll find.

You cannot change others, you cannot control what others will do or say. You can only learn to manage your emotional response by bringing yourself into an aware state of acceptance by being with what is and then directing your focus toward a good feeling place. This is the law of attraction in action, be deliberate. We are creating all the time consciously and unconsciously, so the more you're aware of your internal state the more you can bring yourself into alignment with your vision. You can come into reconciliation with anything that is impeding the path thereby liberating you to generate and focus on your intent in the moment.

Define what another is saying so that you can understand where they're coming from.

The body has no recollection of time or space; it is only at the effect of each moment. But we can become more aware of the patterns that hold us in bondage and we can become alert to find a new feeling or way of dealing.

Respond not over-react!

Fear is a catalyst for growth, for us to move from humanity into divinity. Find Every Awesome Reality (F.E.A.R.) is a pathway to a new understanding of that which stands between what you have and what you want.

Listening: listen to yourself; be an outstanding listener for others; breathe to keep you in the moment of presence; be an active listener.

What we say is just as important as what we don't say; it is all a communication that leads to the unraveling of our path.

Power, not force!

I cannot force anyone to change. But what I can do is observe the very thing that is presenting itself as an annoyance or inconvenience for me, and resolve it in myself.

Open your eyes and see that all these limitations we impose are self-inflicted, because the freedom you seek is always within reach.

The truth really does set you free and even if it's only the discovery within yourself, this alone will heal the pain we create for ourselves.

It's never about the other person; it is 100% about you.

Possess nothing, enjoy everything.

Can we manifest our fears? Absolutely, however this is nothing to fear. Our fears represent the F.orgetting E.very A.wesome R.eality in which we live...so a fear realized shows us the opposite of what it was we truly want to create.

Forget everything and remember.

We are here to remember the essence of our being; we are here to remember to play; we are here to vibrate and energize one another; we are here to learn. Fear is our opportunity to encounter our excitement. All I have to do is be willing to feel, deal and allow the path to reveal what is in accordance with Divine will, and then play…. Enjoy the glory of the grace and ease, and let opportunity be all I can see.

7

SELF-DISCOVERY

"The most common way people give up their power is by thinking they don't have any."
~ Alice Walker; African American author and poet.

"Your greatest challenge is to not be distracted by that which happens in front of you, or is pulling on you or calling to you, but instead to find your center and magnetize to yourself all those things that are in alignment with your inner being"
~Sanaya Roman

"Love just happens. Nobody thinks about how to love, or when and where to love. Nobody is rational about love. Rational thought hinders love. Love is a sudden rising in the heart. Love is an unavoidable, unobstructable longing for oneness. There is no logic in this. It is beyond logic. So do not try to be rational about love. It is like trying to give reasons for the river to flow, for the breeze to be cool and gentle, for the moon to glow, for the sky to be expansive, for the ocean to be vast and deep, or for the flower to be fragrant and beautiful. Rationalization kills the beauty and charm of these things. They are to be enjoyed, experienced, loved and felt. If you rationalize about them, you will miss the beauty and charm and the feelings they evoke. Sit by the seashore. Look at it. Feel its vastness. Feel the rising up and down of the waves. Feel and be amazed at the creation and the creator of such magnificence. What good will it do you to rationalize about the ocean?"
~Amma

We take ourselves so seriously!

Ever wonder why we do that? I mean, life feels like it's all or nothing at times, we place so much stock in having our desires met immediately. We put so much pressure on ourselves to accomplish things in a certain time frame that we'll practically run someone over to make our deadlines – the key word being 'dead'! We will fight to the death to get what we want, and sometimes that death ends up being our own. It's like life, as we know it will end unless we get really intense and serious and insistent.

Well, I'm here to say lighten up a little, things are gonna get done and you can either do it with stress and intensity, or you can sit back a little and enjoy the ride. It's like cooking in the oven: you put the food inside and you know approximately how long it will take; you're not sitting and staring at the food while it cooks, you're happily doing other things and perhaps you occasionally give it a glance, or poke and prod it a little. This is life. We put things in the cooker and they need time to cook. If we're always hovering over, insisting it cook faster, what does that accomplish? We know that everything has its boiling point, no need to rush it, just figure out how long it will take.

In order to enjoy what's ahead, you have to settle in a little. You've planted the seeds, now let them grow! Stop overwatering your life with unnecessary problems. Life is what you make it, so add some honey to your recipe, sweeten things up a little, turn the heat down – it may taste better that way! Let the seeds grow, tend to them with care, observe what they need – not what you think would make your life easier. Remember a time when you feared losing something, and then it happened? Remember feeling devastated? Feeling like life had stopped? And yet somehow life went on, and you were a little beaten and battered, but stronger for the lesson. And when you look back on those circumstances, you might say to yourself: "Wow, I'd sure handle myself differently now! I really made things seem worse than they were!" There were times when you lost love and thought you'd never find it again – but not only did you find it, it just kept getting better!

Life is constantly changing. People are constantly coming into new awareness, inventing new ways and methods, to move us forward with more ease. In order to have the life you choose, you have to lighten the load, take the pressure off everyone you're blaming for your unhappiness. You call the shots – and if you don't like how it's cooking – start over, or give it more time, or find another way to make it how you like it.

It has to start with you first. Lighten the load inside of you, and then you can hash it out in the kitchen and find just the right combo with others, to find a happy medium in relationships. So stop for a moment when you're in the midst of a crisis and pan out to the bigger picture. Maybe even cut to two scenes later! Weigh out all the possible scenarios and ask yourself: what matters most right now? What am I gonna feel later? And in order to feel better later, shouldn't I start with my moment of now? If I'm really wanting something, then I might get it by kicking and screaming – but do I have to feel so awful and stressed and get in this tense, uptight, worried manner or can I soften a little and let things ride? Can I slow down some, make a little space for it all to settle in and melt the awesome different components together to have my final outcome?

What's important to me? The people in my life, and how I see the world. If I sit in gratitude for what I have then I'll get more of what I'm grateful for – more of the fun, wonderful, delicious moments and treats of life. Lighten up. Try doing the opposite of what you'd normally do when you're pressured and strapped for time. Pretend it's already OK – and you know what? It probably will be! Have the courage to try new ways of addressing your intense seriousness; take a breath; if you don't get your way in this very second, then what?

Accept, allow, accentuate

Accept, allow, accentuate as you surrender. In order to have easier, lighter ways, I've found that we must accept our circumstances as they are. You can't change where you're at presently, so this is your first step. Accept what is, without judgment about its correctness. It doesn't matter if it's right or wrong – what matters is: what will you do next?

The next step is to allow what is. If things are unfolding in manner that displeases you, resisting will only make it worse and fighting against it will escalate the situation. So stop, and surrender. If you want your way, fighting against another, trying to prove your point when they clearly have an opposing view, will get you nowhere. So surrender to what is, accept it, allow it, and then you will automatically be able to remember how to handle things with more grace, with your divinity leading the way.

Ask yourself: Do I really want to go down that dark road or do I want to create a new pattern, a new solution? I saw a movie recently, where the heroine couldn't beat her opponent – he was too strong for her. So she surprised him; she took him off guard and kissed him! In the midst of it all, you can stop yourself from that next impulsive act, and ask: Is this really the step I need to take to get what I want? Is hurting another either physically or emotionally really going to make me feel better about me? Will they succumb to my wishes after this abuse? The answer is likely to be no. So when you're confronting anything that seems like an imposition, you have a choice as to what you will do.

Sometimes I stop, and I can see that I could avoid a fight – but my ego is so wounded and I'm so wanting vindication, that I carry on anyway, to relieve myself of all the hurt I feel inside. I know that I'm going to dump all my pain on someone else, and I'll do it anyways. The aftermath is always messy and I know I'm going to have to clean it up. I could have prevented the extra pain and drama had I held my tongue and swallowed my pride. Changing the old pattern isn't so easy to do sometimes, when you're looking to feel liberated or have it your way.

But if you remember your dedication first off is to love – and to love especially yourself – then you will get very good at accepting, allowing, surrendering and remembering what is, and you will tune your dial intentionally to the station that pleases you. Or maybe you'll get up and walk away. No matter what you do, remember it's all in order for you to feel good about you. Life delivers a lot of things we judge and don't like and wished were different, but fighting 'what is' only creates pain inside of you. Handling it, stepping outside the box for a moment, taking a bird's eye view – and you may just decide that it's not worth the pain and you settle in. If you're ever in an accident, the way to escape injury is let your body go loose. The same applies to your mind; if you're stressed, you're likely to break something!

Capture your essence

Distil what it is you want people to see in you, and see it in yourself first. The world is only an echo of the vibration you emit – your essence – which is the sum total of the signals you emit. I believe essence is the way in which the world feels you out. I describe my essence as vibration, radiance, energy, and playfulness. I want the world to see me as vibrant, powerful, bubbly and effervescent, with a passion for life. What is your essence? How do you want the world to see you? In order for the world to see you, you have to know what it is.

Do you even know who you are? I think as humans we all ponder our existence, by examining the physical and investigating the non-physical. The evolution of man is a mystery – but does it matter? Is there such a thing as universal truth, where the answers are never disputed? Perhaps there is, but life will continue to present you with some sort of duality, where you will have the awesome honor to stand in your personal truth and decide what you want to believe.

If you want to believe that purple dinosaurs fly, well maybe they do in some alternate reality or universe. Proving it to others won't make any difference to how we feel about it ourselves. I've spent years trying to convince people to believe in what I see and what I know to be true, and I encounter all sorts of opposition. If the other person doesn't have it within their scope to believe something outside of what they can see, then there's no point pushing the point! Much of what I see and speak about is the unseen, and if the experience is a feeling or a knowing, this cannot be quantified or explained – it can only be interpreted and shared as my personal truth.

One man is a Christian, another a Jew – can they both be right, or are they both wrong? In my estimation there is no wrong, there is only personal choice as to how you want to spend your days. We need to stop having to prove we're right. All we experience is ourselves and that means we are here to see life through our own experiences. How do you want to experience life? It's not for me to judge you in your ability to perceive happiness or even feel happiness. It's up to me to hold a neutral space and celebrate whatever takes place, and for me to encourage myself to follow whatever guidelines feel right to me.

I had a teacher in Jerusalem, Israel, who was teaching the Kabbalah and he said: "We are human beings turning into human becomings." What will you become is up to you! Follow your heart and know that some may assert an opposing view, but what matters most is how you feel about the choices you make, in achieving and feeling your own bliss and happiness. Let others worry about what's right for them. Stand strong in your knowing that life is bringing to you the experiences that align with your being and your life's lessons. Listen, watch and learn. This is the game of life… Play, play, play!

Change: does it really happen?

And should you have to? Don't change! Or change if you want to. Change is such a funny word that we (over) use to blame others for why we don't have what we want. Well, if you just changed, then life would be peachy! Now some say that change doesn't exist, that we can't change and that we aren't here to change. We're just here to remember the 'essence' of our being. Once again it boils down to your personal truth and getting over the semantics. Let's not get caught up in the words, let's find out what change implies and what remembering implies.

We are here to unveil the most authentic version of ourselves – and sometimes that lies underneath a lot of pain fear and protection.

Earlier I spoke of acceptance, allowance and surrendering – now let's add one more: remembering. If we accept, allow and surrender, then we will surely remember. What are we remembering? We are remembering that divinity is at the core of our miraculous beings. As we remember, we are changing the patterns we've learned that have kept us separate from the Divine. We are here to be our personal best self. For many it may seem dull and boring and for others it may seem like a constant adventure. Whatever it is for you, however you are living today, know you have done your personal best to this point. I strongly believe if we could do better, we would. I knew better for years, and I still couldn't get off my perpetual, insidious, blaringly loud hamster wheel with speakers that narrated every one of my repetitive moves.

We are liberating ourselves by remembering, and changing at our own pace. After having experienced working with biofeedback for four years followed by a shift in my neuropathy with Deeksha, I've concluded that we do need assistance in clearing the pathway in order to be all that we can be. The shedding of years of patterns and misery may take time, but if you're willing, then day-by-day you'll be able to identify opportunities and make new choices. Every little bit counts – even if you just re-language you life a little to support being a happier individual, by not using 'don't' and 'have to' before every sentence you speak – this can create dramatic change.

Many would dispute this: many would say, well we keep doing the same thing over and over again. Well, maybe we do know better, but we can't do differently unless we're presented with new choices and solutions and the tools that are essential on the path to evolution. I cannot do something if I don't know how to do it! Many are not willing to learn, and for others it may require a lot of time to learn, but they are at least attempting to do new things. Change happens little by little, and it takes deep dedication. You can change a pattern of behavior in 40 days, so it takes discipline to stay oriented toward the goal – and once again it boils down to choice.

If we are demanding change, then we must educate and commit to time intervals for change, and know that if we could do it any sooner, it would be done. Only in the last four years of my journey have I been able to make more significantly noticeable leaps and bounds. Having said that, I'm not sure if I changed the root of my being or if it's still the same; but I did remove the things that were blocking me from being my authentic self. I've learned acceptance, I've learned to forgive myself for being a creature of habit, I've learned to deeply appreciate and honor life and its inhabitants, I've learned to slow down, be present, play more and enjoy the ride –

even if it is a roller coaster. I'm always awash with deep emotions and thrills and even moments of deep inner stillness. I'm willing to be my best self and I'm willing to not be afraid or embarrassed to expose my humanity as a gateway to help the rest of the world, and as I do this, I grow.

I have learned who I am by putting myself into experiences of pain so that I could be sympathetic to the world and really discover the common denominators of what works from person to person. Of course, each person is an individual, but the blueprint remains generally the same. Change is the only constant; everything is always in flux.

We can do anything

There is a myth that says we can do anything. We can accomplish things beyond comprehension – we cannot fly, but we have devised machines to allow flight. So anything is possible, yes? The myth is that truth is subjective – and here you will have to decide for yourself. Are we here to be punished, or are we here to enjoy heaven now, and the afterlife...after? What you do today affects tomorrow, and if you so choose, live the life you crave and work toward your afterlife – or not.

I love Jesus Christ and I grew up a Jew – but that does not mean I'm no longer a Jew, or that I've converted. I accept and appreciate all the teachings that encourage love, understanding, forgiveness, oneness and pleasure. It's not about the system or structure you choose, it's about the structure that best suits your inspiration. I would never say a happy man isn't happy because he doesn't do it my way. Thank god he does it his way. My way works for me and this book has been written to dispel the illusion of a form or format; it has been written to encourage you to find your unique style, inspiration, commitment, dedication and love inside of you, that moves you to share another day of contemplation, growth, expansion, awareness and joy.

1. The realization. I've realized change happens, it's always happening and not to be attached to another person's change. Be aware of the changes or shifts that need to occur within you and do the work from the inside out. The only way people will ever be what you want them to be is by being it yourself and then you can recognize its form in others

2. Remembrance. Remember, awaken, enliven to who you are: the perfection of god's creation. You have to remember that god fashioned us and we will tick without any effort, but we must fuel and maintain in order to enjoy and stay strong.

3. Is it too late to change? I've found that I haven't so much as changed as grown with awareness as to what I wanted to be all along. The blueprint remains the same, the core values and ideology is there from a very young age.

4. Speaking what you are…is it limited? Defining who you are imposes a limitation on your subconscious. Be aware of who you've been but remember, we are always reinventing ourselves, and being attached to titles can limit our expansive nature. Who you were is only one of the many things you are, so continue giving yourself permission to be nothing or everything. Strip away what identifies you as you, and then see who you would be. Perhaps you find you're just a good person, or maybe you have beautiful hands; whatever it is, it's not what makes you loveable or valuable. You are eternal life force embodying a vehicle in order to play and to understand the limitations of who you once were. If you want change then you have to eliminate titles,

judgments and the like, and be your today, your promising new tomorrow. You will only pay for whom you've been if you keep it as a point of focus and reference. Some cannot get over their past while for others the past is irrelevant. It's your choice what you focus your attention on.

CHAPTER SEVEN SUMMARY:
SELF-DISCOVERY

1. Lighten up a little, things are gonna get done and you can either do it with stress and intensity, or you can sit back a little and enjoy the ride.

2. Life is constantly changing. People are constantly coming into new awareness, inventing new ways and methods, to move us forward with more ease. In order to have the life you choose, you have to lighten the load, take the pressure off everyone you're blaming for your unhappiness. You call the shots – and if you don't like how it's cooking – start over, or give it more time, or find another way to make it how you like it.

3. Try doing the opposite of what you'd normally do when you're pressured and strapped for time. Pretend it's already OK and you know what? It probably will be!

4. Accept, allow, accentuate as you surrender.

5. Accept what is, without judgment about its correctness. It doesn't matter if it's right or wrong – what matters is what

will you do next.

6. If things are unfolding in manner that displeases you, resisting will only make it worse and fighting against it will escalate the situation. So stop, and surrender.

7. Life delivers a lot of things we judge and don't like and wished were different, but fighting 'what is' only creates pain inside of you.

8. Distil what it is you want people to see in you, and see it in yourself first. The world is only an echo of the vibration you emit – your essence – which is the sum total of the signals you emit.

9. If the other person doesn't have it within their scope to believe something outside of what they can see, then there's no point pushing the point!

10. We need to stop having to prove we're right. All we experience is ourselves and that means we are here to see life through our own experiences.

11. "We are human beings turning into human becoming's."

12. Let's not get caught up in the words, let's find out what change implies and what remembering implies.

13. Know you have done your personal best to this point.

14. We are liberating ourselves by remembering, and changing at our own pace.

15. Every little bit counts – even if you just re-language you life a little to support being a happier individual, by not using 'don't' and 'have to' before every sentence you speak – this can create dramatic change.

16. If we are demanding change, then we must educate and commit to time intervals for change, and know that if we could do it any sooner, it would be done.

17. Change is the only constant. Everything is always in flux.

18. This book has been written to dispel the illusion of a form or format; it has been written to encourage you to find your unique style, inspiration, commitment, dedication and love inside of you, that moves you to share another day of contemplation, growth, expansion, awareness and joy.

19. Be aware of who you've been but remember, we are always reinventing ourselves and being attached to titles can limit our expansive nature.

20. Who you were is only one of the many things you are, so continue giving yourself permission to be nothing or everything. Strip away what identifies you as you, and then see who you would be.

21. Some cannot get over their past while for others the past is irrelevant. It's your choice what you focus your attention on.

8

BEING YOUR OWN ORACLE

"Thoughts of your mind have made you what you are and thoughts of your mind will make you what you become from this day forward."

~ *Catherine Ponder*

Words to live by:

1. You are your best authority of what you think and feel in accordance with how you will deal. The choices that present themselves are new in every moment. If you base your future on your past, you will continually draw on your past experiences rather than creating a new outcome by expecting a new outcome.

2. Being your own oracle means having insight and foresight into a larger plan and trusting the voice within to always align you to your purpose with the right people, places and situations for the highest good.

3. Witness, observe.

4. Purposeful Action - be purposeful.

5. Reinvent yourself daily. Try something new every day. If you're in a rut, then do the same thing differently than

you've ever done it before. Take a new route, eat new foods...change can be the catalyst for achieving the life of your dreams. If you're a shy person then initiate a conversation and see where it goes. If you're a super outgoing person, go somewhere by yourself and sit quietly and observe the silence. If you're an extremely busy person, create something just for you, take part in a cooking class, a workout routine, a morning mediation, or read a book – something that requires you to pay attention to the upliftment of your well being. If you're a busy mother I invite you to take a few hours a week to pamper yourself and appreciate who you are and what you are sharing. Make self-care a daily practice, even if it's something small, like giving yourself a treat because it will make you happy. Acknowledge your efforts, big and small – it all counts. No one is counting but you can make all you do have meaning and the things you want to do become meaningful enough for you to create the space to participate. And always remember to take good self-care.

6. Hang out with your fans.

7. Dying for love vs. living for love – feel into that!

8. Love what you do to get to doing what you love!

9. You are your best oracle – be the authority of what you think, speak and feel.

10. Healing is a feeling. Be real with what you feel, and it will reveal what you need so you can deal.

11. Be the Walking Miracle.

12. Follow Your Bliss.

13. God has uniquely equipped each one of us with the tools for building our own empire.

14. "Live a life of Thriving not just surviving. " -Jim Carrey. It's a mindset.

15. Repetition imprints the mind.

16. Lead by example.

17. Create solutions to life! There are never problems, just opportunities to resolve. Figure out the problem by changing your perception and the problem now becomes opportunity to gain deeper insight and awareness.

18. The answers lie within. Become quiet and step inside. What you seek is seeking you, so follow your inspirations, let them become inspired actions to play the game of life without attachment not knowing where you're headed. You will eventually arrive so enjoy the ride along the way; it's all that matters at the end of the day.

19. Jesus Christ said, "When two of you agree, it shall be done." It is the law of agreement. It is almost impossible to see clearly for yourself: that is where the healer, practitioner or friend is necessary.

20. Remember that you have the ultimate say in what is right for you. Others assist us on gaining clarity and insight and strengthening our resolve to make momentous leaps forward. However if you are not complete with something or someone because there is still wisdom in the process,

then surrender to that flow. It will bypass the mind and enter into your heart. You will know with certainty what to do if it truly aligns to where you are in each moment, and you can always change your mind later. The later change may occur because you have now liberated your mind and what resonates now can appear.

What you did before may have been steeped in old belief systems; when you get current, so does everything around you that is attracted to you. When you step in and up to align with what is the divine plan then you know with certainty there is a plan for all in the deeper understanding of perfect timing. You are right where you need to be now.

CHAPTER EIGHT SUMMARY:
BEING YOUR OWN ORACLE

You are your best authority of what you think and feel in accordance with how you will deal. The choices that present themselves are new in every moment. If you base your future on your past you will continually draw to your past experiences rather than creating a new outcome by expecting a new outcome.

9

PROSPERITY

If you look at what you have in life, you'll always have more.
If you look at what you don't have in life, you'll never have
enough.

~ Oprah Winfrey

Living in a land of longing.

Are you a person who is always longing for something different? Is the grass always greener on the other side? Do you fear commitment?

What will it take for you to settle in to what you have and be where you're at? How can you achieve more when you struggle with what you have?

I've worked with many millionaires who, contrary to popular opinion, live in scarcity and lack more than the average person who has much less. But when we speak of lack and scarcity, it does not only refer to money, it also refers to your consciousness. There are people who have so much, yet lack so much as well. They are constantly struggling, and in the land of longing they have forgotten to value what they do have. They are always focused on attaining something better for their fulfillment. They have lost appreciation for all the abundance surrounding them and they want more.

The irony is that in terms of money, these people thrive, but internally, they suffer and yearn. Prosperity is a state of being. You could have two nickels to your name and be so rich that the universe pours out its abundance to you, and you know nothing other than good fortune. Poverty is a state of being as well. Americans are probably some of the richest poor people in the world. We don't even realize how much we have; we're so abundant that we've become numb to it. Granted, it's wonderful to have all the fun toys and to be able to buy whatever you want when you want it, but do you depend on physical things to bring you joy, or does that one physical thing accentuate the joy you already feel inside? The United-State (a term coined by Dr. Sarah Larsen – www.DrSarahlarsen.com) is the unification of whichever state we choose to live in.

Wealth is knowing how to see the richness all around you. If you stood in nature and looked around you would know you were royalty – it is so beautiful and plentiful. Do you stop to smell the roses, or are you rushing through life and not noticing the little things? Do you say thank you and mean it? Is your life centered on how much you have or on how much more you need before you are happy? Are you enjoying the ride along the way or are you impatient to arrive at your destination?

Is scarcity running you ragged?

You don't have to be poor to be ruled by scarcity. I've made a very strong claim to life and that is to never define myself as poor or broke. I am not a broken person, nor am I a poor person. No matter what I have in terms of money, I am always so filled up. Just because your monetary means don't always reflect your soul, does not give you the right to reaffirm what you don't want. If you want a life of more, saying you are less only affirms the focus on the less. Worrying about not having is just the same as saying you don't have it. When I'm in times of financial transition I say: "It's not within my budget at this time", but I never affirm that I'm broke or poor – because that is a lie.

I'm surrounded with so much that even in my darkest hour no one could ever call me poor. Now, that's not to say that not knowing where money will come from is not on my mind, however I have too many demonstrations that prove to me that I am always in abundance. Abundance can only improve as my consciousness elevates and as I make more space in my life to receive my birth right to love, fulfillment, abundance and happiness.

Money is love and love is energy.

So all we're ever exchanging in life is energy. What form of energy do you like to share? I once read a book that said money was love, and from that day forward my whole perspective on life and money changed. Up until that point currency was a way to attain the things I desired; I never saw it as an exchange of energy. When you have to pay a bill or buy something, don't view it as a life-depleting event. When I decided that all I was exchanging was love, my life dramatically improved. In fact, not only did I prosper more but I also enjoyed the benefits of giving and receiving love (money) all the time. So here goes: if you view currency as energy and energy is neutral and you take this neutral energy and define it as love, then whenever you're paying for something with currency or receiving currency – this is just another form of love in your life, sent from the Creator.

So your day becomes one big love fest and instead of dreading those bills, you can say: "oh now I get to share my love, and in sharing my love more love will be returned to me because what I put out always comes back to me a billion fold."

When someone pays me for my services, they are giving me a form of love. When I buy groceries and I give the cashier money, I am handing them units of love. All day my intention goes toward giving and receiving love. This is one way to begin to source more love and money into your life, especially if your relationship to money to this point has been one of fear, lack, longing and struggle. This could shift the way you view the world. And if love is money and money is love then all we want for others and ourselves is to prosper in order to share more of the love currency. One of my clients paid me by check, and in the line to describe the transaction, he always wrote 'units of love'. I delighted every time I received a check from him, and he delighted in writing the check because he felt the value in what he was exchanging and it was infused with love from both ends. Now you can run around perceiving money as love and share it all day and no one has to know what you're doing, because it's about the energy you are feeling inside. And if your intention is to share love then you make a point of it in every transaction throughout the day.

CHAPTER NINE SUMMARY:
PROSPERITY

1. Prosperity is a state of being

2. The United-State is a term coined by Dr. Sarah Larsen www.Drsarahlarsen.com and describes the unification of the state we choose to live in.

3. If you're wanting a life of more, saying you are less only affirms the focus on the less.

4. When I'm in times of financial transition I say: "It's not within my budget at this time", but I never affirm that I'm broke or poor – because that is a lie.

5. Money is love and love is energy

6. View currency as energy and energy is neutral and you take this neutral energy and define it as love, then whenever you're paying for something with currency or receiving currency – this is just another form of love in your life, sent from the Creator.

7. Love is money and money is love then all we want for others and ourselves is to prosper in order to share more of the love currency.

10

CHANGE IS THE ONLY CONSTANT

How wonderful it is that nobody need wait a single moment before starting to improve the world.

~ Anne Frank, writer

"Change your expectancies and you change your conditions. With the realization of success, we receive the gift of success, for success and abundance are states of mind. No man gives to himself but himself, and no man takes away from himself but himself. The "game of life" is a game of solitaire; as you change, all conditions will change."

~ Florence Scovel Shinn

Embrace the pace in order to feel grace.

When we live in opposition to this concept we are fighting against the current, and swimming upstream. Life is always handing us circumstances to manage or address, and while one may mimic the other they, are all unique in their own merit. We can never assume another's position in life nor expect that another should adopt our position. We are co-operating to share in our unique ideas and as we move along we find people who are in alignment with what we believe life to be as our current reality. Those who are in opposition to our view will appear on our path as well and it is up to us to remain open, flexible and observant of what we are encountering. If we were to embrace every experience as it comes, we would prevent friction in our relationships, as we would have no expectation about how another ought to behave. We are there in participation and observation –

and most importantly, we are there to serve, uplift and share what we are.

When I embrace what is, and surrender to what will be, I am now in the current of grace unfolding. I know god is always conspiring on my behalf to provide the correct people, places and situations for the highest good that align to my divine purpose, mission and intention. And since my intention is set for interactions that will benefit me in my ever-growing, ever-expanding awareness, then I know no matter what I encounter, there will always be a blessing, a refinement, a helpful insight into better relating with myself and others in all my affairs.

Viewpoints.

Life is dependent on your view of what you think it is. Is life a party, or is life hard? This example is taken from a Tony Robbins conference I attended. This subtle distinction (party or hard) can be all the difference in your world as it moves you forward, creating a better, more responsive supportive reality. If life is a party how would the world be different according to you? If "life is like a circus" what may appear on your path now?

If, like many, you have been taught and reinforced that life is hard then it make sense that life seems to be hard! Because as you know – what we focus on expands in all directions.

If at the base of your foundation you believe fundamentally that life is hard, then don't you think that life will show up for you with constant difficulties? And if you constantly re-iterate and re-enforce life is hard then your vocabulary will take on a similar suit and tone. You will use disempowering words and phrases that constantly substantiate your point of view. Such as: I'm stressed, it's their fault, this is hard, I can't, I don't want – all of these words continue to drive home the point life is hard. Now, you have a case for yourself proof and evidence to boot. As you see reality, so becomes your reality. We are witnessing life, and life is subjective to every individual, as we are all standing from a different vantage point. Now what would it look like if you were to decide right, here right now, that "life is easy, fun, and full of opportunities"? Would you potentially take on a new energy, would your tone change? Would you use inspiring phrases? Such as: I can do anything, I have a choice, I embrace what appears, I am loveable and worthy of abundance, I am worthy of amazing, supportive relationships, and so on.

Two points of view – what will you choose?

Is it really easier to blame others for how we feel and constantly put ourselves in harm's way? We do this by making excuses, pointing the finger, being controlling, uptight, rigid and judgmental; by taking offense or being defensive; by convicting and evicting people from our lives because they don't meet our standards because we have set up rules that impose limitations, disconnection and fear, based on wanting significance, love and approval. Who are you to think you know what's best for another? Isn't it all just an opinion, and doesn't every individual have to come into their own determination ultimately of what works for them? What works for one doesn't work for all. Even in this book! I write these words as an invitation to look at things from a new or different point of view, then it's up to you to determine what works for you personally.

Daughters and Fathers.

So I found myself in a situation in the last few months where I was encountering daughters and their fathers. Since I haven't yet had children myself, I can only advise from my personal experience of being a child and from the understanding of human principles that make sense to me when it comes to relationships. I have a tendency to be very outspoken, and given the nature of my work, I can sometimes blur the lines, offering my opinion when I am either not asked for it, or in situations where I just feel like sharing. I've gained valuable insights into myself this way, as I have found myself asserting opinions and discussing opposing views on how a parent parents a child.

From this I understand that when it comes to families it's very important to advise the advisable. If someone is not paying me for my services, then stepping in, even with the best intention, even with a desire to share tools that will inspire or transform someone – is not my duty. It's best not to interfere, because that implies I know what's best for another. If I have consent from a parent to offer advice, then what I say may or may not be taken to heart, but at least the information is given from a place of neutrality to better serve one and all. Unasked, I am both judge and judger.

To illustrate my point: I was driving in the car with a friend and his daughter. The daughter asked her father what she should do if a guy wants to talk with her, but she didn't want to talk to him? The father responded: "Tell him to "f^&k off."

At first I thought, wow that's harsh. I suggested that she find a polite way of terminating his interests, along the lines of, I'm involved with someone else. But the father interjected: "No, that's lying and that won't work. Just tell them to f^&k off."

In the heat of the moment, thinking I was in a safe zone of banter, I again expressed what I felt, saying: "Don't listen to your father," and continuing to advise the young girl. I felt that any man deserved better than to be aggressively dismissed. I felt that I was in the right, and inwardly I celebrated my amicable way of teaching. But the father yelled at me, and threatened to evict me from the car. He was really triggered and I was shocked at his reaction. He continued ranting, and then the penny dropped – this is how my father speaks to me!

It suddenly became clear why my interaction with my father follows a similar pattern, and I could see how I instigate this pattern all the time. I also came into deep insights concerning men in general, and then on a personal note, I saw what was necessary for future involvement with me, that I could actively choose.

Create your every moment.

In every moment of our life we have creative control. We are in charge of how we feel. "All we experience is ourselves," said my teacher, Dave Cowan. Therefore all that exists is inside me.

We are learning to merge the conscious mind and the subconscious mind to bring into harmony what is possible from the inside out. We are gathering data and information as we go to "inform" ourselves of what we are in total. We are a total compilation of our past experiences, imprints and learned perceptions and responses.

Communicate Clearly

Is life always giving you feedback? Or is life a constant barrage of attacks? Are you in the offensive state or defensive state? Or are you on the sidelines being an observer? Do you even have control of the direction in which you're steering your life?

If we were to know that at any given moment, we could shift into a more effective style of communication, then we may give up the need to excuse our inadequacies or talk of the problems we've had. We'd speak of the opportunities that evoke our courage to confront the uncomfortable, voice our preferences. No preferences are wrong – they are exactly that, a preference; one preference does not negate another when a choice is at hand. If you are offered chocolate or vanilla and you choose chocolate does it mean you are rejecting vanilla? No it does not. It means you are choosing what delights you in this moment.

Communication styles

I asked my friend with the daughter, what he does when he feels conflict in relationships. This is what he said: "I walk away." I countered with: "Well, what about finding a solution or gaining insight into why there is conflict with another?" I will paraphrase his response as: "I walk toward the people I like being with."

Well, in truth, in order to walk toward you have to also walk away. I didn't push the topic but I do feel there is value in having a discussion or an argument; there is value in discord because it brings our attention to our behaviors and how we are interacting. If I am a novice at something, I may fumble to begin with and it may take me a few times to really see what it is I am doing that is working, and not working, in order to improve. This is where making distinctions comes into play. If I continuously encounter the same form of lesson and have not learned how to respond in a way that feels satisfying, then I will continue to draw that experience into my field, so that I can gain deeper insight into how to handle myself.

We confront every situation with the data we have accumulated prior to this moment – so we can only respond from a place of awareness of what we have attained now. Wisdom comes from compiling new information and reassessing each case individually in the moment it occurs. I can only do better when I know what better looks like, and what it feels like. We never intend to harm or insult others, it just happens; and then we get feedback as others can see what we are doing and share how it makes them feel. From that we can make adjustments to future relating.

I've come to realize in my line of business that you can never make assumptions about how people will respond; we all have different communication styles, just like we have so many dialects and languages. In order to speak the 'universal language of love' and be heard even without words, we have to listen and know when what we're saying is perceived as feedback, an interaction of joyful banter, or perceived as judgment and attack. We have to really determine where a person is at in their evolution and find the words to reach into their hearts. If I'm in college and you are in 1st grade I won't be discussing quantum physics with you. I may however demonstrate the effects of this no time space continuum by playing a game with you that illustrates my knowledge or perhaps I will just share my love. Either way I'm not imposing the years of study and information I've accumulated onto a child who is developmentally in a different space. I know my audience and I act accordingly. The same goes for our interactions with our peers. If there is something you would like to share and you are uncertain of the response, you could ask if that person would like to hear your feedback or would like new information. From this place you have extended an invitation as opposed to a forced concert with closed doors and no exits.

Now in the heat of the moment you may be unaware that what you may say may trigger another person; we are all coming to the table fully loaded with our stuff, so we don't know when that chord may be struck. You may say something that sounds very similar to that person's former partner, and now you've unleashed a cannon of pain, judgments, fear, feelings of lack of self worth and the like. Now they are responding to you from this place and have displaced their emotions of association on to you. "Blame is displaced pain," says Dr. Sarah Larsen.

What do you do to discharge the situation? Sometimes there is nothing you can do but walk away. You could ask to have a discussion with the other person and ask how they are feeling, or you could ask, what could I do differently in the future to create a smoother interaction if this were to occur again? Remember before entering into a place of resolution, two people have to be on board – it's a mutual affair. Sometimes the only thing to do is let time pass so both parties have time to reflect upon their actions. I know in the heat of the moment forcing an interaction with someone who doesn't want to interact only leads to deeper discord. You must resume a place of love and acceptance for all parties involved but most importantly yourself. If you could have done it better you would have. We are an impulsive, reactive species by nature, so aligning yourself to a practice of loving despite what you gain in return is the goal. It's like yoga – every time you go to the mat you will feel different. You may make incremental improvements while you strengthen and become more at ease with each pose. This is life.

Communication and honesty can be the very thing that saves the relationship because there is humility when you admit that your intentions were good but the implementation went awry. This is where patience is essential. Patience is key to ever expanding awareness for the strength of perseverance.

It's not about the other person understanding you it's about you understanding yourself by coming to each and every relationship willing to see what appears. If an underlying creed is I don't want drama in my life then you may try to avoid it, you may block it or even walk away when it appears, blaming the person who brought you the drama. You then make it about them, saying, they just don't get it. The truth is – you're not getting IT. The IT is that what you resist persists. Walking away from conflict or avoiding being emotionally stirred is an impossibility as long as you are human vacillating in duality and interacting with others. Now if you have come into being in-light enlightenment then your perceptions of your interactions will not yield the suffering and you will be able to observe your environment and find how you are always in a co-operation and co-participation with others and the creator. Therefore all actions are right action and you find what benefits you from every person you interact with.

Lack of communication verbally is still communication, not to be mistaken for assumptions and making up stories that you think you know why others behave as they do. You can only look at yourself and see what you are noticing about how you show up in the world and how you want to show up in the world. Remember all you experience is yourself, therefore if you like what you see it is you; if you don't like what you see it is you. We hate to admit to being at fault or wrong or causing an emotional response in others, but the truth is we are in "come-unity" in our world and in order for us to merge into deeper "come-unity" we have to make the distinctions when we are in separation, lack, judgment and out of love.

Make Inquiries.

So often in life we make assumptions because the writing is not on the walls, and we assume that if it's not stated then it cannot occur. However all it takes is a simple inquiry to find out what's possible.

I was at dinner with a friend. He had ordered a lemonade and I wondered if they did refills. He responded: "No, I don't think so, there's nothing written that indicates there are refills." I didn't take that as the last word on refills! I was thirsty and so I asked! And the first refill turned out to be free!

This goes for everything in life. We make up stories in our head; we let our minds wander, we wonder and assume, all the while silencing our inner voice from being heard, out of fear or a limited mindset, or some form of confining behavior.

The expansive state of attraction is just that– expanding in all directions, and inclusive. So if you think something is true, why not ask before assuming? There is also another way we live in this assumptive state, where we think that how we perceive or define certain behaviors or words are, across the board, the same for one and all.

Here's an example: My father would often say to me, "Don't lecture me." Now after so many years I finally stopped in my tracks and thought to myself – I love this man, I'm here to share with him and every time I open my mouth he comes back with the same remark. Perhaps I'm not clear what his definition of 'lecture' is. I would never do something to intentionally harm him and I certainly want to grow myself in awareness, so I asked him: "Please define what this means to you, because obviously I don't understand. My father replied: "You need to be more like your sister; she just kicks back, never says a word and just goes with the flow."

So in order for me to encounter my father in a new fashion, I would have to become a better listener, because when he speaks he just wants to be heard, not to be challenged to look at another point of view or to be informed of my opinions. Now I know you might be saying – that's a very one-sided relationship; it's very conditional. What I would say is: do you want to be loving or do you want to be right? In every relationship there is usually one person who has a better understanding of what is really going, of being able to read the subtext behind every interaction. If I were to genuinely understand what my father was saying, which is, I interpret what you are saying as a criticism, and understand that he is personalizing what I say and that there is already a lingering feeling of offence that just repeats itself every time we interact, then I would understand that my father wants to feel good about himself and that when he sees me and I say or do something, he already has negative associations with me. He will blame me for the feelings that linger inside of him, because he hasn't come to terms with the fact that I cannot approve or deny him – and vice versa – and this is where we continually run into conflict.

We are both wanting to feel good about ourselves in the other's presence, but the subtle expectations and fears arise and lead to discord because in the moment neither of us are capable of identifying the deeper emotional need from past interactions. We vibe it in. We can never offend or do the wrong thing to another because it is always just an interpretation that is occurring according to that person's value system and rules they have set up for themselves. We enter into oneness when we can love the other as they are and not be affected by what they do or don't do, because we truly understand the principles; nothing is personal, not love nor hate. It's just an experience we are having; we love when we ourselves are in love with who we are. And we hate when we are in separation and in judgment of behaviors others are demonstrating by rejecting and denying those behaviors inside ourselves.

We can't always account for the trigger or moment of offence as it usually happens so quickly; we may feel like we're falling down the rabbit hole, out of control. If that's the case then the only way to be out of control is to let go, look at what's occurred and see that what you are experiencing is mimicking something from your past. See where you may bring insight into identifying repetitious patterns in all your relating and relationships. It's usually a much bigger offence that has occurred over and over again and perhaps takes on different forms, yet it's all the same source of origin. That source of origin can distil down to this: either you are in love, ready to be love in action toward yourself or others, or you are in separation, making judgments and distinctions because of a perceived lack and a need to attain something from someone else to validate who you are because you do not validate who you are.

So if you are in love – real love, the type of love that is unconditional, asking nothing in return – then there can never be a problem, there can never be anyone to blame, no-one can give you significance as you are already signifying your own existence. You don't have to beg or plead or force others to see your point of view as it matters not if they agree or disagree, because you know that this love you extend says: I accept you as you are. Now you may not agree with people but that does not have to prevent you from celebrating what they themselves celebrate with in themselves as their personal truth. You have an opportunity to share what you believe, however if there is no audience to receive it, then how can you find a way to turn yourself around and celebrate the choices of those around you.

Informing others.

I went to my mechanic today to check on my headlight. He started to share how he believed his daughter in law didn't know enough to be a nutritionist and he felt she was too skinny and that she needed to grow up and leave people alone and not try to enroll them into vegetarianism. Now for many years I was a vegetarian, so I was chuckling inside – not out of superiority like I knew something he didn't know, but because I realized we create our own perception of reality. It's not about changing the person; it's about informing the person. They can change their own perception by stacking enough evidence to prove themselves correct in any direction. I said to him, well you have a point – look at you, you're 76 and super positive, you glow, because more importantly than what you eat, it's what you think. If you think like shit then you have to be aware of the shit you put in your body, because it's all about balance. An alkaline state can occur from not only what you put inside nutritionally but what you put inside energetically, verbally, emotionally. So I said, it's perfect how you are, because it's clear it's working for you. I did not negate him and try to enroll him in my education; instead, I supported him in his education. Now if he had expressed interest in knowing more about what I meant by alkalinity of the blood, I may have recommended something for him to read so that he could inform himself and come to his own understanding.

I've met people whose diet is equally as important as what they are thinking and I've met others whose diet has no bearing and it's all about their psychology. One particular client is remarkable; she glows, her faith with god is unquestionable and ironically she eats whatever she wants, parties when she wants, and it seems to only fuel her beauty, because she does it with a liberated heart. She does the internal, emotional, psychological work and she is aware of herself and her growing opportunities. So while I've recommended an alkaline lifestyle for many of my clients I know that when she is ready she will naturally move toward the things that empower her body temple. Today she now feels inspired to go deeper and put substances to the side; she is ready for more support, but she could only come to this realization on her own. I never made her wrong; I encouraged her for all her unique individual choices based on the moment as it was always calling for something new. Sometimes it required beer and smoking, sometimes it required colon cleansing and working out, loading up on water and greens. Wherever she traversed it was always the perfect thing in that moment, as it always led to ever-increasing awareness and expansion. She continues to glow and grow and she has really come to know the truth for herself – that love in all directions given can transform everything.

In-joy the journey

The journey is your every moment. Like I've said before, it's not where you're going, it's how you feel along the way. Confront what appears on your path right here, right now. In-joy the journey – be the journey, allow the journey, embrace the journey, create the journey. The journey does not always have to be enjoyable because sometimes it is just what it is. We determine its value and meaning. The journey is just an expression to say BE HERE NOW! The journey is the fun along the way to discovering yourself. The destination never arrives because as you journey through life you will always have a new goal in your sights of realization. As you arrive, another goal appears, and the journey continues.

There are moments when I feel so deeply satisfied – when I accomplish my list of goals – and then when that's complete, new ones appear. Life is ongoing and the joy is the exploration of the unknown. We can make life an adventure if we so choose.

Moving forward and the use of language

Whenever I would fixate on the past, a dear girlfriend would say: "…and moving forward'. I use it constantly with others and myself when I want to signify that what we're doing is moving forward in life. The journey is progressive and steady and we can be assured of growth, as all things do. Whenever I listen to someone in their story and the energy becomes stagnant or redundant and it seems like they are a hamster on a wheel turning and turning and arriving nowhere, I chime in and say: "And moving forward, what would you like to create next?"

Asking what someone wants to create next allows him or her to focus on the positive twist to whatever it is that they are saying they don't want to create. Author and speaker, Esther Hicks (Channeling Abraham – a collective consciousness) teaches that the universe does not know the difference between what is good or bad – it only knows your point of focus. So when we choose our words, we want those words to spawn the creations of our choice.

What is it you want to create? Are you speaking in words that inspire the upliftment and growth of who you are remembering yourself to be? For example, growing up, my father would always say, "don't be late". And so with that directive, I was always late! In fact it became a problem over the years, because as soon as I heard those three little words, my whole body would start to react and I'd feel sick. Even when I'd try to be on time, something would always delay me. I hated showing up late. The few times I was on time, my father would say: "Well at least you weren't late." But the tone was derogatory and I never felt good about myself even then, because I wasn't greeted happily – I was greeted with the idea of failure, no matter what I did. At least this was the belief I held for myself.

Now let's just see: how does it feel when someone says: "I look forward to seeing you on time." This implies celebration, success, love and encouragement! So I realized that the reason I was never on time and the reason my father could never say it differently was also part of my story and creation and fear. I held a belief that I needed to perpetually feel bad about myself, and part of that was finding ways for my father to reaffirm that I wasn't good enough. He needed to affirm that my actions were an indication of how I felt about him and others – that I didn't respect him and value his requests. Well, when I realized I no longer wanted to be at the affect of my fears and I realized I was the source of this collaborative creation, I changed the pattern within me and I accepted that my timeliness had no bearing on my lovability. This had been an excuse to stay in separation but now I wanted to celebrate myself and celebrate my father. I shifted my belief, and when my father said: "Don't be late", I would say: "Don't be late!" instead of reacting and getting defensive – and showing up late! Instead of focusing on my lateness, I started focusing upon my ability to be timely; that I deserved to share this time with my father and that spirit would make way for me to show up on time.

I realized I didn't need to react to him and get upset, and that really all this fighting over time was a by-product of me seeking love and approval that I needed to give to myself first. The fighting over time stopped; in fact, I stopped fearing it all together.

And I very confidently, easily show up to see my father in a time that works for both of us. I understand that it is an honor to share space with my father, not an obligation, and that we come together to celebrate one another.

Change your wording, change your life.

When we language our life according to what it is we choose and how we want to feel, life can deliver us just that. And since the universe does not know the difference between what we're saying we do or don't want – it only adheres to our point of focus and vibration, then it behooves us all to speak clearly what it is we want to participate in. And of course the opposite applies – know what it is you're not wanting because in the contrast you can claim and receive what it is you are wanting.

Example: Do you say: "Don't forget the orange juice," or "Thank you for remembering to get the orange juice"...see the difference?

I take a lot of time to be very deliberate with my words, as I believe life is a constant prayer and what we speak can shift our reality in an instant. So communicate clearly with deliberate intention to have and receive your exclamations and proclamations as you command the universe you choose to live in.

What would life look like if...

God is within you allowing for you to hear and see the signs that will lead you to the highest choice for the path you focus your attention upon the most.

I genuinely believe that when we have entered into the flow, we are listening. Everything smoothly sails from one interaction to another. The wisdom of the divine mind aligning for you at all times as the subset of your belief system will yield just that – a remarkable timing. It flows you from where you are to where you want to be with beautiful nuances. Recognizing and attuning your awareness to deeper insights and refinements that you can incorporate into changing your perceptions to a fluid flowing reality of surrender, grace and ease.

If you are one of those people who constantly affirms how hard and stressful life is then I can only imagine your perception of life would continually bring you seemingly hard and stressful situations, to show you that what you believe is true. You substantiate your reality. It's a choice to perceive life and define what we are experiencing as stressful. That word is so commonly used to define something we undergo that creates emotional disharmony, we have become addicted to saying how stressed we are, how hard things are. It's perception, granted it may be true that going through a move, a separation, a divorce, a death, sickness, fighting, etc. are all stressful events, however it is up to you how you want to respond to what's appearing on your path. Are you the victim to your circumstance or the creator whose stance is to take lemons and make lemonade? All these experiences are material for growth. Being upset is part of life, just like pain, just like love, joy, the absence of love, and contrast. We all live it. What would life be without it? Perhaps it wouldn't be as fun, but you never know, that's just a story I could be telling myself or perhaps we wouldn't know those signifying great moments if we didn't have those hard moments to make a distinction of preferred reality or preferences. I'm not here advocating one is more right than the other, it's just variety. Ultimately when you come into love with what you experience and you come to accept things as they are then you could probably find joy in the hardships as you would realize – it's just an experience.

We want to judge, we want to make others wrong, to possess, to claim significance, to personalize and taint things to our personal truth. We want to blame others for our pain, we want to claim our greatness, love with no bounds, we want to live the life where we feel good and we have certainty that we will find the resources we need to be something in life, to have value. We depend on others for our value, for our love. Without connection we are nothing and with connection we can become everything. However the connection starts with you, going within, getting to know the terrain of you, finding out what makes you, you. Who do you model your life after? What are your influences? What excites you? What annoys you? What do you run from? What do you say to yourself privately when you are alone? Do you spend time with others and focus on others to avoid yourself? Can you sit with what is and not make yourself wrong or others wrong for not having the proper tools to do the job? Can you look in the mirror and see yourself clearly as a perfect child of god? Can you understand you are an evolving being who has been influenced to believe in something that perhaps you haven't even explored yet, because you're afraid you'll be rejected or you'll reject yourself? Could you risk looking at the truth and face yourself and recognize that you are part of a higher intelligence that connects to one and all that moves the ocean and raises the sun upon each new day? Could you stand in your own power and recognize that you are a miracle walking and that whatever you have done, whatever you have been, you can be new today?

What would it look like if you could forgive everyone including yourself for all the times you forgot to love, and were living in fear? If you let everyone off the hook once and for all, if you flushed all the stories, burned up all the nonsense and assumptions; if you understood that all the stories you made up about yourself not being loveable, are part of the greater whole. What if you could know that today was brand new, this moment is all that exists, and you could decide what's next? You could just give love without fear of being rejected, you could trust yourself and your connection to the universe because you could remember that god is supply and that no one has power over you, you get to determine how your reality is set. Your foundation is one that is built upon a knowing an implied love, respect, trust for one and all because that is your point of focus. From here life delivers to you the very thing you focus upon. Anytime you experience the contrast to that it shows you where you forgot to be this love in action, trusting the universe to supply what is necessary based upon your focus and what you've asked for consciously and subconsciously.

That is why you are reading this book to learn practical applications to aligning your conscious and subconscious mind to know thyself.

When you have a system of knowing the self, you are empowered to experience life for what it is, simply by trusting that you will be delivered your bounty daily – just like you never question the sunrise and sunset. When the sun shines upon you it never asks anything in return, it does it knowing it will do what it's suppose to. It gives its rays freely and even if there's a fog layer that covers the light you know it's always they're shining. That is what we are, we have the capacity of the sun to shine our light, sometimes we have a marine layer covering our light but it is still there. So we must know that we are always that light, we all have the capacity to shine and we do it everyday – even if it rains we are always there in the brilliance of our light. This is the contrast, the variety of life, to remember that sunny days don't always mean better days; it's all in your perception. The sun offers and when the sun sets there is now another light that emerges, but somewhere around the world the sun is shining and continually moving to kiss its sunbeams across the planet. The moon follows and there is never true darkness as there is always something illuminating our "system". If the moon wanes there are the stars, and their light is equally as powerful, yielding its own unique energy transference.

So you see we are always being illuminated with light, with mystery, with power, with contrast, with beauty.

If you could remember you are this miraculous light energy form being that came into existence from the union of man and woman, and is still one - what would be possible then? Could we not then pardon and forgive our fellow man for forgetting his miraculousness? That while he may sit in darkness and think that this is his life, the switch is always available to him if someone could remind him how to find his way to that light. We are here to share, connect, inspire, uplift, and remind love. Life can be hard, challenging and hurtful – but love is not hurtful, it is the absence of love that hurts because we are formed from this one love union, the reconnection, this polarity merged. We are comprised of light and dark and this is what creates the balance. What would the world be without the contrast of day and night? It's so exciting that we live in contrast and we can enjoy so much variety from the clothes we wear, to the cars we drive, to the foods we eat, to the plants we see, to the flowers, to the birds and the bees. What a marvelous world full of beauty. Are we able to see the beauty in the sewer system? Can we see the benefits of how everything serves us in contrast to what we think life should be? The sewer benefits us because we all have waste and it needs to go somewhere. It goes for our experiences and stories, we allow for the experience of what is, there is beauty in your perceived negative contrasting emotions too. We digest, we assimilate, then we eliminate, we repeat this process constantly. However the only constant is change, therefore habituate yourself to knowing that in every moment our cells are alive, they hear us, they respond to us, they work with us. We can instruct our bodies to generate emotions both good and bad, we can imagine, we can think, we can feel, what a gift to touch, to smell, to taste, to hear. Stop for a moment; let's see how we can change our perception for that annoying traffic jam into gratitude for the movement, for the opportunity it provides. Appreciating that we even have a vehicle to sit in traffic with. Everything has a benefit, even the arduous painful things. Can you see it? Are you looking? Today is a new day! What will you do today to improve the quality of your life? To improve your relationship with yourself? What makes you feel? What makes you feel good? What makes you feel bad? It's remarkable to know thyself. Spend time in inquiry, what am I feeling? What am I seeing? What would I like to be experiencing? Take those notions, those emotions, and get creative, you can do it right here, right now. If you don't ask you wont know! Be interested that makes you interesting.

Detaching from our concept of time.

Time is of the human mind…god did not create time, god simply created the recognition of one day to the next. My affirmation for you all is: "There is always enough time to have the experiences of your choice or choosing."

Recovery time.

Take time to adapt to the changing times, especially when you make a large leap of faith to achieve your dreams. People can usually get up, brush themselves off and move on to the next thing – but as time goes on and you repeat the same offense over and over again, the recovery time can change. It may require more time to accept that you continually put yourself in harm's way. Maybe you've repeated the pattern so often that this time it took out a few more parts! So instead of a day in the shop for repairs, you have to call out and order parts, and what used to take a day to repair takes three because you keep bashing in the same fender. And now it's weakened, and needs a complete overhaul. This is usually the impetus for change! It's almost like we have to experience a total overhaul before we'll do something different.

I had a friend who was always dating a different woman; he had no time for drama and long painful relationships, so he used to say "NEXT" and mean it, and move on. Well, words to live by! He's now married with his second child on the way. He never got caught up in what wasn't working and continually made space to meet his match – the one that felt like "Oh, now it's time to park!" I believe that in life, you'll know when it's time to move on. If you're a person who can endure a lot of pain and suffering it may take you longer than others – and this is perfect for your path. I've always been extremely loyal and forgiving which is not the best breeding ground for my friend's theory of "NEXT!" but as I've learned to love myself, my choices are currently based on the enjoyment of having experiences and showing up for the witnessing of that.

If I show up with that attitude I can repeat the same lesson and my vehicle won't end up in the shop at all, because I've equipped myself for roadside service! But in many cases those days in the shop just may be what you need to finally get up the courage to say "no more" to what you don't want. Time to drive in a new direction! Once you determine how it is you want to feel, and what it is that would bring you your highest fulfillment and excitement, you can begin to send those "rockets of desire", as Abraham says, and await the responses and surprises.

Allow recovery time, allow yourself to be surprised and be open to leaving the old, by eagerly saying "NEXT!"…Bring on the next new passenger to join me on my ride! I'm ready to be surprised with the ingenious ways that god's will is blended with my creative mind.

CHAPTER TEN SUMMARY
CHANGE IS THE ONLY CONSTANT

1. When I embrace what is, and I surrender to what will be, I am now in the current of grace unfolding. I know god is always conspiring on my behalf to provide the correct people, places, and situations for the highest good that align to my divine purpose mission and intention.

2. As you see reality, so becomes your reality.

3. In every moment of our life we have creative control. We are in charge of how we feel. "All we experience is ourselves", therefore all that exists is inside.

4. Communicate clearly.

5. There are no wrong preferences – they are exactly that, a preference and one preference does not negate the other when a choice is at hand.

6. I can only do better when I know what better looks like, what it feels like.

7. We have to really determine where a person is at in their evolution and find the words to reach into their hearts.

8. I know my audience and I act accordingly.

9. If there is something you would like to share, however you are uncertain of the response, you could ask if that person would like to hear your feedback or would like new

information and to learn something.

10. Remember before entering into a place of resolution two people have to be on board, it's a mutual affair. Sometimes the only thing to do is let time pass so both parties have time to reflect upon their actions.

11. It's not about the other person understanding you; it's about you understanding yourself by coming to each and every relationship willing to see what appears.

12. Lack of communication verbally is still communication, not to be mistaken for assumptions and making up stories that you think you know why others behave as they do.

13. Remember all you experience is yourself, therefore if you like what you see, it is you, if you don't like what you see, it is you.

14. So often in life we make assumptions because the writing is not on the wall, and we assume that if it's not stated then there is no possibility. I you don't ask, you won't know.

15. The expansive state of attraction is just that – expanding in all directions, and inclusive.

16. Do you want to be loving or do you want to be right?

17. It's not about changing the person it's about informing the person so they can change their own perception, by stacking enough evidence to prove them correct in any direction.

18. Be the journey, allow the journey, embrace the journey, and create the journey. The journey does not always have to be enjoyable because sometimes it just is what it is. We determine its value and meaning. The journey is just an expression to say BE HERE NOW!

19. The universe does not know the difference between what is good or bad – it only knows your point of focus. So when we choose our words, we want those words to spawn the creations of our choice.

20. Life is a constant prayer and what we speak can shift our reality in an instant. So communicate clearly with deliberate intention to have and receive your exclamations and proclamations as you command the universe you choose to live in.

21. When the sun shines upon you, it never asks anything in return, it does it knowing it will do what it's suppose to. It gives its rays freely and even if there's a fog layer that covers the light you know it's always there shining.

22. Life can be hard, challenging, hurtful but love is not hurtful it is the absence of love that hurts because we are formed from this one love union, the reconnection, this polarity merged.

23. ."There is always enough time to have the experiences of your choice or choosing"

Allow recovery time, allow yourself to be surprised and be open to leaving the old, by eagerly saying "NEXT!"…Bring on the next new passenger to join me on my ride! I'm ready to be surprised with the ingenious ways that god's will is blended with my creative mind.

11

EMPOWER YOUR LIFE

"A lot of people are afraid to say what they want. That's why they don't get what they want."

~ *Madonna*

Empower others. Empowering others empowers we. How can we do this?

My number one objective in life is to learn how to celebrate people for where they're at, and where they want to be. In order to do that, you must start with your own inner journey. It begins by taking that leap and swinging from experience to experience in anticipation of feeling and seeing new perspectives in all that is around you. Empowering others is the highest service you can share in life; it means you see everyone's potential and you encourage the realization of achieving their greatness. Every day is improving as a society, as people are catching on to the necessity to be more giving and allowing of others.

Be a person who empowers others by being an example of empowerment. An empowered person takes charge of their life with dedication, faith, appreciation, celebration of life's events and a willingness to always improve and refine themselves and the lessons they learn day to day.

Steps toward empowering others:

- Celebrate people's efforts even if it's not how you would do it. There is wisdom in all behaviors and actions, and an opportunity to learn something about yourself.
- Have faith that the Divine mind is operating to benefit the greater good of all.
- Smile.
- Be present.
- Listen.
- Offer your time.
- Notice your surroundings.
- Be grateful for the honor of participation, all of it, whether bliss or pain.
- Tell the truth first and foremost to yourself so you show up authentic in who you are.
- Inspire people by being an example.
- Accept people as they are.
- Be understanding of people's timing – every pot has its own boiling point.
- Find something you love in everyone you see.
- Confront the resistance and let it be, in fact go toward it and see what it can show you.
- Change your perceptions of yourself and others.
- Use life affirming words like "I can".
- Focus on what you do want.
- Trust yourself. This creates healthy parameters by knowing what you will and won't tolerate inside of you;

then accept what you resist and watch others act in accordance with what you have addressed within you. It starts with you!

· Release yourself of boundaries and being bound to a state of being; this way, you'll experience what you are inherently inside of you.

· If it doesn't come naturally then be intentional to embrace those parts you judge and resist.

· Be responsible and personally accountable for your life.

· Breathe more consciously.

· Have the courage to feel your feelings and make them known.

· Be patient with the process.

· Check in with yourself often by taking inventory.

· Have awareness to any hidden motivations.

Romance can be a lifestyle

Be the lover to the world you live in.

I'm a hopeful romantic. I love love, I live for love, and all I ever want to do is make love to everything I encounter and if I'm out of that groove then I'm in fear and separation. I've forgotten to stay in my heart and in my body and I'm at the effect of others' pain and suffering.

If I'm not making love and being a cupid to all I see, then I've forgotten my mission on this planet. We are not all alike, however, and most of us would love to make love to life in every moment, but it's a challenging thing to do when we get caught up in what's not happening and we lose track of all the good that has happened.

Romance is a way of being with yourself and the world. Romance can be buying you a treat; noticing a change in someone's appearance and gifting them with a compliment. Romance can be the recognition of the beauty that surrounds you. Romance isn't just a candle-lit dinner for two. It can be the recognition of your mother who lovingly serves you and does your laundry, or the husband who goes to work each day and brings home the groceries.

It can be that tender kiss you plant on the one you love. It could be the silent moments where you don't need to speak and all is understood. Romance is a way of being toward your universe; it's the appreciation, the passion for all things living and inanimate. It's the ability to see clearly and know you are your own living, walking, talking being with choices. Romance can be the time you take to write a thank you to someone you love, or the flower you bring to his or her doorstep just because. Romance is capturing the essence of life, living life to the fullest, and being super present to what is. Romance is a person who considers your comfort before theirs, who will make compromises and sacrifices to see you smile. Romance is not taking anyone for granted, instead offering your admiration for what they do for you – like the cashier or the man behind the deli counter.

Romance is recognizing that every moment is precious, so don't delay in expressing what you feel to the ones you love; don't hold back from expressing awareness of the love, the joy, the fun. Don't delay in always offering yourself gifts, if it's a hug, a kiss, a wildflower on the side of the road – a whiff of nature's gold. We are surrounded with a life force that asks nothing in return but that you open your eyes and admire it with all your senses. Pay more attention to your surroundings, look up more, look down more, walk slowly and really look around, stop and listen with your eyes closed so that you can hear every syllable being pronounced. Find something beautiful in front of you and focus on that until it becomes you too. Be romantic with your kids, with your neighbor, with your fellow workers…be sharing and caring and pay attention, do kind considerate things that show you are present.

The chaos will always be the hustle and bustle of the day, the ins and outs where most of the time it's about serving the world – so serve yourself by noticing what works and celebrate life by giving love in return. The more you love and celebrate what is, the more life becomes sweet and exciting. If you want more romance in your life, create it from within – don't make others responsible for giving you pleasure. Pleasure yourself and it's inevitable that you will always have pleasure arriving at your door. If you love roses and no one brings them to you – give them to yourself and know that it is a gift from spirit to you. You have the means to be luxurious, so take the time and get curious – let the world show you how loved you are.

People want to connect, they want to feel the romance of newness all around, so step out your door and try something new that is romantic too.

Tips to live by

1. The destination of your direction is a one-way path forward. Take the direction of your life by using this statement: "In moving forward, what would it look like if…. I were to have or create or experience x, y, z…."

2. Or just moving forward and reorient you to that new focus.

3. Separation is an illusion of the mind, just see what is there, nothing is ever what it appears to be, look beneath the surface and know that aloneness can swiftly turn into all

oneness when we accept ourselves and what has been.

4. Life can be unpredictable, infuse it with intention and deliberate action that will quell the heart of the unknown, turn the mystery into an exciting undiscovered journey.

5. When something is closed is it your opening.

6. There is no such thing as exclusion because what you focus on is inclusive all the time. Ester Hicks, who channels Abraham, says it's all inclusion "When you give your attention to something that you desire and you say yes to it, you are including it in your vibration. But when you look at something you do not want and you say no to it, you are including it in your vibration. When you give no attention to it, you do not include it, but you cannot exclude anything that you are giving your attention to, because your attention to it includes it in your vibration, every time, without exception." ~Abraham.

7. We are always reinventing ourselves, because we are comprised of data – as you delete one file you make room to upload a new file.

8. Gossip pains the soul because you are only ever experiencing the embracing or rejecting of yourself.

9. Longing for anything reinforces the lack of not having.

10. Do it because you are choosing it. You never need to justify why you choose things that seem irrational – it's your individual path and process.

11. Your physiology changes your psychology…Tony Robbins. Change your body position will change your disposition.

12. The focus is on balance not on perfection, life is a practice not a perfect, we are always moving toward equilibrium.

CHAPTER ELEVEN SUMMARY:
EMPOWER YOUR LIFE

1. Empowering others empowers ourselves.

2. Celebrate people's efforts even if it's not how you would do it. There is wisdom in all behaviors and actions and an opportunity to learn something about yourself.

3. Release yourself of boundaries and being bound to a state of being, you'll experience what you are inherently inside of you

4. Romance can be a lifestyle. Romance is a way of being toward your universe; it's the appreciation, the passion for all things living and inanimate. It's the ability to see clearly and know you are your own living, walking, talking being with choices.

5. If you want more romance in your life, create it from within – don't make others responsible for giving you pleasure. Pleasure yourself and it's inevitable that you will always

have pleasure arriving at your door.

6. There is no such thing as exclusion because what you focus on is inclusive all the time. "When you give your attention to something that you desire and you say yes to it, you are including it in your vibration. But when you look at something you do not want and you say no to it, you are including it in your vibration. When you give no attention to it, you do not include it, but you cannot exclude anything that you are giving your attention to, because your attention to it includes it in your vibration, every time, without exception." ~Abraham, through Esther Hicks.

7. Your physiology changes your psychology...Tony Robbins. Change your body position will change your disposition.

8. The focus is on balance not on perfection, life is a practice not a perfect, we are always moving toward equilibrium.

12

DREAMS

"I believe in pink. I believe that laughing is the best calorie burner. I believe in kissing, kissing a lot. I believe in being strong when everything seems to be going wrong. I believe that happy girls are the prettiest girls. I believe that tomorrow is another day and I believe in miracles."
~ Audrey Hepburn, actress

We all have a blank canvas to create our dreams on.

When in doubt imagine it out. The best way for us to get what we want in life is to create vivid images that depict the energy, situation and emotion behind that which we are choosing to put our attention on. Only in our ability to see it can it take form. The unimaginable becomes the attainable as you give life to the creation you are wanting to see and experience.

Here is an exercise in creating what you want:

Imagine you are looking at the story of your life from front to back. It's a large book with so much content – all the sorrows, the excitement, the adventure, the ups and the downs. Now in your mind's eye, imagine flipping to the last page. Grab a pen and write 'The End'. Circle the words with a heart and underneath write: 'Thank you'.

Imagine a bookshelf, and on this bookshelf is a gap, just the right size for your book. Shelve your book, and then forget about it. You have read and re-read each story in this book until you are word perfect. In order to create a new story you need to have a blank canvas; you need to start anew with awareness and deliberate intent. (Note: this book of your life to the present is a place of reference, not a place of habitation for this current moment.)

Sitting next to your old book is a brand new book. Open to the front page and write: 'The Beginning'. This is your opportunity to begin creating a new life, as you weave magic with every word you write, full of life, meaning and a deep sense of knowing that if you can imagine it, it now has the opportunity to become real.

You may begin the new story of your life like this: "I am joyously receiving life today. I am filled with love and gratitude for all that I've achieved and will continue achieving. I am always aligned with right action, attracting the right people, places and situations for my continued journey for the highest good. I find the blessing in all my interactions. I am continuously becoming more aware and I follow my inner compass to lead me appropriately in order to fulfill my dreams. I trust in God's Divine plan and I actively participate faithfully. I choose love."

We all have unique desires and in order to fulfill our goals and dreams we must be as clear as possible as to what they are. We can more easily navigate our vehicle towards our destination when we have a lock-down on the location. So in creating the next phase of your life, you must let the past go in love and gratitude, and open yourself up to the possibilities that lie ahead. Your success rate in the past does not determine your success in the future; you now have some help along the way, as long as there is willingness and most importantly the willingness to surrender to accept what has been.

You will now begin to attract people, places and situations that support your vision for the highest good! Imagine writing, painting, seeing and discovering all that is within you as you begin to visualize this beautiful picture called your life. In order to embrace each day as it comes, learn how to 'source the force' and be intentional with your mind, body and soul.

This is a planet full of opinions, freely expressed. Whose opinion will you listen to? Who will you believe? What is true? And what applies to you? I have been told many things over the years: I am an alien; a fairy; a star seed. I have been told that I have come to raise planetary consciousness. All of this fascinates me – it's fun to play in the land of possibilities! I have learned to never discount anything – I continually seek knowledge to discover all the possibilities that exist. But at the end of the day I remain faithful to one source and that is the source of the light within, that will always give me choices on this free-will, co-creative planet. Knowledge is power but action is powerful and awareness will inspire faith and faith can inspire a shift in perception. When we begin to see the energetics of our being and we remain open to our own unique individual journey, we will discover the true vibrancy that is within us all and awaken to our core blueprint: that of miraculous beings of source energy which illuminates, maintains and nurtures every one of our cells.

So whatever path you choose, there is no wrong way, nor is there only one way to arrive at your desired destination. The path you choose and how you choose to travel will determine the time of your arrival. If you're a person who feels more comfortable staying close to the earth, staying grounded, you may choose to drive or take a train; but if you're someone who needs to be places quickly, no time for a hassle or fuss, you may book a Lear jet and get to where you're going fast. Along the way delays might happen, depending upon the agreements your soul made before arriving here. You may just be in for a slower ride, but that's not to say there are absolutes. There is the choice and willingness to participate and you can only arrive when it is truly aligned with the nature of your calling.

"I recommend asking for the right people, places and situations for your highest good to appear in your life to support your dreams." For me this becomes my insurance policy; once I have made this claim to the universe, I am saying that I am actively participating, and I'm aware that no matter what happens, at the end of the day I will reflect in awe and gratitude for what appeared as signposts on my path – these signposts let me know that I am moving in the right direction. My daily affirmation gives me the opportunity to hold true to what is the highest opinion for me. And at the end of the day, I review each event to see how spirit is cooperating with me to fulfill my highest excitement in L.O.V.E.

Inspiration, insight, and illumination.

It is through inspiration that we gain insight into our highest choices. Author and speaker, Jenny Hough, once told me to "take only inspired action as you move through life". Inspired action leads to insights, and once you have insight you can begin illuminating these insights with imagination, which leads you back to your inspired action. Inspired action means if you're prompted to do something, call someone, or create something, that this is the next step to take for you, towards your inspiration. Take delight in watching out for new insights, awareness or observations that come from that inspired action!

Many call this 'following your bliss' – it doesn't matter what you call it, I just want to encourage you to start doing what your inner voice inside prompts you to, every day.

OK, so there are lots of things you want to do, but you don't have the time or the resources to take action. If you're confined by time and space, then at least in your own mind's eye, create an awareness of what it is you would like to participate in, and visualize yourself doing it. Afterwards, you may realize that it wasn't necessary to take any action; all that was needed was to engage your mind to see how it feels. The mind is a powerful tool learn to operate your tool, you can then achieve the desires of your dreams in a more efficient deliberate manner.

Remember who you are.

I often hear people in the New Age community say: 'Remember who you are.' I never thought this was worth listening to! I can't remember who I am, because if I could, do you think I'd be suffering and so unhappy? So what does: 'Remember who you are' really mean? Now I can only speak from my experience, but all you have to do is know that you are the realization of love united in form. You are the miracle of creation. You are the majesty of all of divinity; you are vibration, you are energy, you are perfect creation.

I am really asking you to awaken to your divinity, which puts L.O.V.E. before all things. It puts L.O.V.E as the center of it all. I believe our hearts are the anchor between heaven and earth, and it's our duty to remember that there is a loving force that sustains us all. Remembering your divinity and caring for your heart will lead to consciously creating your life with inspired action in L.O.V.E. So remembering is about going inside and recognizing the magnificent of your existence in human form. We are all walking miracles and it is easy to forget this when we're caught up in a war between the heart and mind. In remembering that we are humanity and divinity united, we then can begin to have compassion for the struggle of man in his duality and begin to embrace life with more awareness. We can admit that there may be things on this planet that we do not subscribe to or even believe in, but we know that we're all here for our own unique unfolding of life, whether you experience it as such or not!

So in remembering who we are, we can validate others for their viewpoints based upon their own learning curve. Only when we can embrace the duality of our nature can we truly awaken and remember the purity that exists within us all. Only then can we infuse L.O.V.E into all we do daily, to disperse and dispel the fears and erase the lines of separation and celebrate everyone for their own personal exploration. Remember to L.O.V.E and you will begin to remember your conception and miraculous materialization into form.

Ambition creates the dream.

Have you ever heard someone say, "Well, he just isn't ambitious enough, that's why he hasn't succeeded yet?" For me, the word 'ambition' is often taken out of context and manipulated to mean something entirely different from its true form. Ambition is the knowing and motivation required to achieve a goal or dream. But ambition isn't the only component necessary; it also takes dedication and commitment.

I have always seen myself as ambitious, but the problem wasn't in my ambition – I had plenty of that! The problem was taking action to realize my ambitions. Many obstacles presented themselves on a daily basis, and until I learned some mind control, balance, and commitment I was incapable of achieving my ambitions.

If someone tells you: "You have no ambition" – listen and then define it for yourself. You may find that you have plenty of ambition, but you haven't identified what it is you want to invest your energy into yet. Or you may have obstacles to overcome before you can pursue those ambitions.

Exercise: what are you ambitious about? Do you have any obstacles that prevent you from turning your ambition in to action? Once you've identified the obstacles, i.e. fear, current job, lack of money, etc., what can you do to overcome, release and re language your life to align with your goals?

Respond rather than react.

What's the difference between a person who responds and a person who reacts? A person who reacts is one who never pauses before they launch into an answer; there is no deliberation or consideration about what comes out of their mouth! Most of us are in constant reactive mode, but in order to have more harmonious relationships, you might have to practice the art of responding rather than reacting. Take a beat, a pause before you answer. Really ask yourself – is what I'm about to say truly how I feel, or am I just saying this to be defensive of my ego? Am I genuinely speaking my heart and truth as I know it in each and every moment?

When you take the time to review or pause before you react, you may be able to prevent serious confrontations. I was hiking with my father once, and things started to get heated and reactive. I decided to take a beat and ask myself what action I wanted to take next. I chose to continue to be reactive, but I did it with awareness; that awareness started to open up a new way of being for me. You may take a beat and see yourself saying the most horrific things; if you can, stop yourself mid-sentence and ask yourself: "Will this really achieve my desired outcome? Will I get what I want this way?"

You may decide that it feels better to yell and scream and beg for what you want. That's not wrong, but the power behind responding rather than reacting is that you take the time to be deliberate in your participation in life before you act out of impulse. Or you may find that you can bypass the blame / victim / perpetrator scenario and move into love and compassion. You may find a new way to express from your heart instead of your egoism head – where entitlement lives. Whatever the case, make it a practice to feel before you speak in situations that trigger your reactive human side. You may find that just taking that short pause and really identifying what it is you want in any given situation may prove to be invaluable in actually attaining it.

The more aware you become of your reactive patterns, the more you can prevent the repetition of what you're not wanting, and the more you can align within each moment as you see yourself walking down the same path of defeat and stop it in its tracks and make another choice.

Responding requires you to slow down, take a beat, breathe, and ask: "Am I about to create the outcome I want? Does this next comment support me in receiving what I want? Am I coming from my ego or am I coming from my heart? Do I have a hidden agenda in this conversation? Am I seeking love and approval, and is this how I will get it? Am I willing to lose my relationship over defending my right to be right? Can I really step away from what it is I am desiring and remain happy? Do I really mean what I'm about to say? Am I being mean because my feelings are hurt? If someone were to say the exact thing to me, how would it make me feel? What is a more loving approach to this situation? Oh, I've already said so many bad things, how do I stop now?"

Just stop, surrender and ask: "What will bring me to my highest path?" There is always a calm in the eye of the storm; you can stop at any time and find that calm.

Let go of the disasters of your past. When they emerge, feel them and then let them go. Remember since there is no time or space every time we bring up a past memory it can elicit the feeling we once felt; if the feeling has not been neutralized it can catapult the system into responding in the same manner or feeling the same way you once felt before. Use the disasters of your past as reference points of understanding and identifying what was to know what will be.

Blind spots – not seeing what is really happening. The beauty of life is that we continually awaken to our sight daily. We put in a rear view mirror so that we can have a full view of what surrounds us but there is limitation in those mirrors – unless you're willing to turn around you may not see the whole view. People can be the eyes to what we cannot see for ourselves. We all see different things in life. So check in with people around you to see if they are seeing a different version or variation of who you think you are being. When enough people bring the truth to your attention take action to update your system and perhaps humble yourself into admitting that you are still in the refinement of your alignment.

CHAPTER TWELVE SUMMARY:
DREAMS

1. We all have a blank canvas to create our dreams on. When in doubt imagine it out.

2. We can more easily navigate our vehicle towards our destination when we have a lock-down on the location. So let the past go in love and gratitude, and open yourself up to the possibilities that lie ahead. Your success rate in the past does not determine your success in the future; you now have some help along the way, as long as there is willingness and most importantly the willingness to

surrender to accept what has been.

3. In order to embrace each day as it comes, learn how to 'source the force' and be intentional with your mind, body and soul.

4. Knowledge is power but action is powerful and awareness will inspire faith and faith can inspire a shift in perception.

5. So whatever path you choose, there is no wrong way, nor is there only one way to arrive at your desired destination. The path you choose and how you choose to travel will determine the time of your arrival.

6. There is the choice and willingness to participate and you can only arrive when it is truly aligned with the nature of your calling.

7. "I recommend asking for the right people, places and situations for your highest good to appear in your life to support your dreams."

8. My daily affirmation gives me the opportunity to hold true to what is the highest opinion for me. And at the end of the day, I review each event to see how spirit is cooperating with me to fulfill my highest excitement in L.O.V.E.

9. Take only inspired action as you move through life. Inspired action leads to insights, and once you have insight you can begin illuminating these insights with imagination, which leads you back to your inspired action.

10. Inspired action means if you're prompted to do something, call someone, or create something, that this is the next step

to take for you, towards your inspiration.

11. The mind is a powerful tool learn to operate your tool, you can then achieve the desires of your dreams in a more efficient deliberate manner.

12. Remember who you are. You are the miracle of creation. You are the majesty of all of divinity; you are vibration, you are energy, you are perfect creation.

13. I believe our hearts are the anchor between heaven and earth, and it's our duty to remember that there is a loving force that sustains us all.

14. Exercise: what are you ambitious about? Do you have any obstacles that prevent you from turning your ambition in to action?   Once you've identified the obstacles, i.e. fear, current job, lack of money, etc., what can you do to overcome, release and re language your life to align with your goals?

15. Respond rather than react. Really ask yourself – is what I'm about to say truly how I feel, or am I just saying this to be defensive of my ego? Am I genuinely speaking my heart and truth as I know it in each and every moment?

16. Just stop, surrender and ask: "What will bring me to my highest path?" There is always a calm in the eye of the storm; you can stop at any time and find that calm.

13

C.H.O.I.C.E.

Create, Honest, Open, Inspiring, Communication, Everyday

"The question isn't who is going to let me; it's who is going to stop me."

~ Ayn Rand

If we know how to love, we can love each other and may also love the Divine. Love comes spontaneously and has no rules and regulations.

~ Mother Meera

I'm doing it because I'm choosing it!

Life is a daily choice and in order to create the life you choose, you have to actively participate in its happening. It is such an empowering thing to think: "I'm doing it because I'm choosing it." In fact choice gives real value and meaning to whatever it is you share as a couple or in a group setting, when you know that each person is there of their own accord. So whatever you do, do it because you choose it. And if you are doing things that others are choosing for you, you may want to re-evaluate where you have complied with another's wishes.

Remember that many decisions we make today may create perceived obligations tomorrow. For example: a man gets a woman pregnant, but later he feels this deep burden and obligation to the life he's created. In the moment he made the choice to practice the act of pro-creation, he also signed up for its consequences; it was his choice, in that moment. So make your choices with the recognition that everything you do today has a part in your tomorrow. Do what you choose and live it fully! This way your life becomes one amazing opportunity after another, because you're always in personal accountability. And if you do decide to participate in something due to peer pressure or a sense of obligation, you have taken this upon yourself. No one can make you do anything. There has to be a place inside that complies in order to not feel victimized. Many of us do things because we don't want to be judged for our choices, so we do something because it seems right, rather than doing something because it feels right. I suggest tuning in to the feeling and if you're not clear, don't commit; leave your options open. You always have the right to change your mind; it takes courage to assert your truth and risk hurting someone else's feelings. But when you establish that nothing is personal and it's about timing, lessons and preferences, then you can enjoy the leads and guidance you receive and act more courageously as you trust and know that there is no wrong way; there is only learning from every place you participate.

I was recently invited to an event a few of my friends were hosting – a sound healing night. I wasn't really feeling like participating; it sounded good in theory and I did want to support my friends, but every time I asked, I just really didn't feel inspired to participate. I knew I wanted to stay home and write that evening, but the friend hosting the event insisted I be there, in order to activate the potential for more group healings in the future. So I weighed it all up. I felt so honored that my friends wanted to include me, and since one of my main issues is that I'm not included enough, I saw this as a sign from the universe that life was including me and I needed to pay attention. I asked for it and here it was. But on the other hand, with my psychic sensitivities, when I go public, especially to a healing event, unless I'm in a place of truly wanting to share – receiving or giving –then it's better for me to stay at home and stay committed to my projects.

One of my biggest lessons has been to learn how to honor my intuition and follow my bliss. Sometimes I want to do things just because I don't want to be excluded, but when I arrive to many of these events, I see that it was just curiosity that led me there. Sometimes that's OK. But many times I go because I don't want to be left out and whenever I go with this as my premise and hidden agenda, I never enjoy myself, it's not fun for me. So there are two sides of the coin. On the one hand it's always an honor to participate and I always want to be included; but on the other hand, I'm learning how to do something because I really want to do it. If I'm tentative or I'm led in another direction, then I need to follow that lead.

But this time I didn't honor myself. I felt pressured to go and I was not strong enough to stand in my truth and say no. So I went and as usual, whenever there is a sense of obligation, I know there will be a lesson! Something will occur to prove myself right – I shouldn't have gone in the first place – and that in order for me to grow, I have to ignore my inner judgment and suffer the consequences.

So it played itself out, and that night I really experienced the truth for myself. If I attend an event from a place of obligation, and my better judgment is telling me NO! Then I can change my mind at the risk of upsetting others. In the end, this result is less costly than doing something I don't want to do and paying for it later. I now know that the more truthful I can be about what it is best for me, the more I can allow others to be this way too. Then I know and trust that my reality becomes one of flow, acceptance and allowance of circumstances shifting, and that I learn easily to adapt and not take anything personal. I know that something greater will occur that I cannot see yet, but I am trusting that I will be led to my inspired desires coming to fruition.

Rejection is protection. What is not for you will not come to you, and what is yours will come charging forward. It will all be revealed in time. Trust that you will only receive what is for the highest good of your being, and even when you do things out of obligation, the learning is always there and there is always a blessing in every interaction. There are no mistakes. So I've learned every day to go to that which inspires my greatest joy and excitement.

Write new lyrics for the old record you continually repeat.

Life is so exciting! Every day we can find something new that will titillate us and excite our nature and our senses. I love getting new music – it's so fun to really listen and feel the lyrics and instruments reverberate throughout my being.

Have you ever noticed, when you get a new CD, you find that one or two songs just speak the energy of your life, and because it comforts you to know that we all experience the same ups and downs, you'll maybe play that song or songs over and over again. In fact you never tire of the lyrics and you can listen to the song ad nauseum.

However there comes a day when you realize that the words you once loved so dear, that once felt like your best friend who empathized with your highs and your lows, just doesn't seem to fit anymore. But you continue to play the song and little by little, you realize that it just does not please you in the same way – because you are changing and growing.

Sometimes we try to force ourselves into submission, into stagnancy. The song that once seemed so alive just doesn't have the same luster it once had. In fact you've already found a new song and the words to this new song now ring true for you. It's not like you can't still enjoy the old song and the old lyrics; it's just that as you shift and evolve, so do the words that surround you and in order to create the life you desire, you may have to change the tune.

Don't let the intellect direct.

My dear friend always use to say this to me, which I think she took from studying the works of Wayne Dyer, famous author and speaker. And yes I've spoken about using the word don't and for this purpose I found this to be a clever little aphorism to direct you into the heart – because the answer lies in the heart of the matter. The heart needs to be the epicenter from where you ultimately make your final decisions.

Anything anyone says is an opinion.

You make the choice! In conversation, where we are not regulating the flow of exchange, people often share unsolicited advice and opinions. We must remember that everyone has their own perspective on life, one that comes through their own personal experiences, projections and fears. All their ideas on life come through this filter. So whenever you're listening to another's opinion, ask yourself: is the person sharing someone whose values you respect or appreciate? Is what they're saying something that you can really feel for yourself? Does this person have an insight you may have been unaware of?

Ultimately before defending or justifying your case, remember that these assertions are only opinions, and ultimately you make the choice as to who, what, how and when in your life. All anyone can ever do is offer his or her perceptions. It is ultimately up to you how you'll choose to respond in the end.

Get crystal clear on your vision.

Having a clear vision for your life will create the foundation for the construction of that life. If you know what it is that inspires you, and you know the things along the way that will encourage its development, then all you have to do is fit the pieces together, one by one, and rest assured in the completion of your project. Like any good contractor, you must have the idea and the vision and then you must recruit the team to make your vision come to fruition.

Building anything takes teamwork and in life we must remember that we cannot realize our visions alone. We are all playing a part in the creation of all that is. So find your crew and trust in your direction and believe in the project...the only way anything ever gets built is with a vision.

Don't look behind.

Look at what's before you! The past is a place of reference, not a place of habitation; live where you want to be, not where you once were. This is the beauty of life when we move forward; we always have the opportunity to leave behind whatever no longer serves us.

CHAPTER THIRTEEN SUMMARY:

C.H.O.I.C.E.

1. Create, Honest, Open, Inspiring, Communication, Everyday.

2. I'm doing it because I'm choosing it!

3. In fact choice gives real value and meaning to whatever it is you share as a couple or in a group setting, when you know that each person is there of their own accord. So whatever you do, do it because you choose it.

4. No one can make you do anything. There has to be a place inside that complies in order to not feel victimized. Many of us do things because we don't want to be judged for our choices, so we do something because it seems right, rather than doing something because it feels right.

5. But when you establish that nothing is personal and it's about timing, lessons and preferences, then you can enjoy the leads and guidance you receive and act more courageously as you trust and know that there is no wrong way; there is only learning from every place you participate.

6. Rejection is protection. What is not for you will not come to you, and what is yours will come charging forward.

7. Write new lyrics for the old record you continually repeat. As you shift and evolve, so do the words that surround you; in order to create the life you desire, you may have to change the tune.

8. Anything anyone says is an opinion. Everyone has their own perspective on life, one that comes through their own personal experiences, projections, and fears. All their ideas on life come through this filter. All anyone can ever do is offer his or her perceptions. It is ultimately up to you how

you'll choose to respond in the end.

9. Get crystal clear on your vision. Having a clear vision for your life will create the foundation for the construction of that life.

10. Building anything takes teamwork and in life we must remember that we cannot realize our visions alone. We are all playing a part in the creation of all that is. So find your crew and trust in your direction and believe in the project…the only way anything ever gets built is with a vision.

11. Don't look behind; look at what's before you! The past is a place of reference, not a place of habitation; live where you want to be, not where you once were.

14

EXPERIENCE LIFE

"As you love your own body, so regard everyone as equal to your own body. When the Supreme Experience supervenes, everyone's service is revealed as one's own service. Call it a bird, an insect, an animal or a man, call it by any name you please, one serves one's own Self in every one of them."
~ *Sri Anandamayi Ma*

"Your attitude determines how you experience the world."
~ *Sanaya Roman,*

Can you sit in stillness and be silent? Discover who you are through self-knowing and awareness.

Sitting in silence for a few moments each day is critical if you want to become a person who knows one's self. Even if it's for only five minutes in the morning, sit quietly and tune into your breath, into your body. How are you feeling? What would you like to create today? Are you excited about what's next? Asking these questions can initiate an intention-setting process, to create the best possible day for you. Make a point of asking for assistance from your guides, angels and the Creator; send the light ahead, using affirmations to make you feel inspired and encouraged.

Don't rush; take these few moments to set the tone for the rest of your day. Go inside, and see if you already have expectations about the things you don't want! Or are you already tuned into receiving the things you do want? By taking a few minutes before you start your day, if you wake up grumpy, or sad, or anxious, you can begin to do something about it. If you just rush into the day, and don't give yourself the opportunity to address what's wrong, then the day is bound to get worse!

If time is limited, ask: "What can I do right now to improve how I feel?" Find out what is keeping you separate from your joy and from your Creator. You may find that utilizing the tools for the life you crave will assist you in this. If there is no time in your day, then do it while you're in the car, or on the bus. Instead of getting on the phone or listening to music, sit quietly and listen to your thoughts.

When I'm in a hurry I love to fill myself with golden light, or wash my body with the golden light, especially if I'm feeling off. I also ask for any attachments I have to a particular outcome to lift from my being, including people, places and situations as a co-factor in my happiness. The happiness you seek can only come from within you, and while people and situations can give momentary pleasure, when they're gone and you have to be with yourself, how will you weather the storm? Holding on to what you want and fighting for it to happen, never results in a happy outcome. However if you're clear that you no longer want to fight for what you want, and you make space and take the time to position yourself in the vibrational alignment of events coming to you, then you can ease into joyful anticipation for what's coming next.

Wake up in the morning and breathe, and command your day. Know that even if you aren't feeling good now, you can achieve it eventually. Little by little, the more co-operative you become, the more flexible and willing you are, the more the Universe will make a way where there never was a way before. Trust and receive, follow your inner promptings, because believing is achieving. Forgiving will set you free to receive the next wonderful thing that is showing up in your honor, to greet you in the new place you've arrived. Continue moving forward, and you will continue to grow.

Sometimes I question if things can really improve in life, but then I realize that every day I am more knowing and more aware; I settle back and think of the awesome journey ahead! It's taken me this far, so I wonder what surprises await me, and how the Universe will coordinate the next manifestation of my desires for the fulfillment of my joy!

Sugar cravings and other addictions (additions).

Do you desire sweetness in life? I've always felt that addictions are a by-product of needing love and approval in some form. Life is about body balance, but if you are a person who loves to be committed to a certain way, then follow your bliss. I never do anything half-assed, and I always experience whatever interests me to the extreme – all my life teachings have been based on experience as I fully immerse myself in whatever it is that piques my interests.

Balance in the midst of extremity is not an easily attainable place, but my ultimate goal is for the pendulum to swing to the middle. I've done everything from an all-raw meat diet, to becoming a vegetarian, to eating raw foods. I've gone from being extremely free with my body to being celibate for extended periods of time. I've spoken in other languages for months without uttering a word of my native tongue. I've gone from being the biggest talker, to days of total silence. I've fasted, I've cleansed, and I've sacrificed moments of instant gratification for my dedication to certain traditions. I went from being a go-go dancer, experimenting with my sexuality with men and women, to living with orthodox Jews in Jerusalem, covering every inch of my body and upholding their steadfast traditions. And in all cases I found glimpses of happiness.

I went from being a complete slave to cigarettes and coffee, to being completely free of all addictions. I was even addicted to sugar. I've swung high and low my whole life trying to find somewhere in the middle. I use to be that person who always needed attention, and now I just show up giving attention. I use to use my feminine sexual ways to get love and approval and to feel my worthiness; this is the thing I seek least in my life now. In fact I went from needing it all to becoming it all. I have uncovered every one of my idiosyncrasies and this has led to the balance I have always sought. The way to give up my so-called addictions was to emerge myself in them completely. And still today I'm aware that they could all be activated in an instant, should I desire to play out that part of my life again. The last addiction to go was to drama, and this one I need to monitor more than the rest!

But I have dedicated my life to feeling good and if I am to enter into any one of my extreme lifestyles again, I now have more understanding about myself. (My body does not support the pain so I cannot harm myself any longer.) Now that I have accepted my quirkiness, others do too! And when I stand comfortably in accepting who I've been and who I am becoming, then life truly supports my ongoing balanced evolution. It doesn't matter if you have extreme ways of expressing who you are; everyone needs structure within their own system to push them into growth. It's up to you how much and for how long, and to continue to be loving towards yourself as you do it. The more I love the more I want to be good to my body. Everyone's perception of what is good for them will be different from person to person and from culture to culture.

Addictions are by-products of a need to feel good inside. If you love sugar, you want more sweetness in your life; make a note of how you could be sweeter to yourself. If you don't like sweet things, set an intention for love; sweetness cannot harm you, it can add to who you are. I'm not advocating for you to go against your dietary needs, but gently suggesting that you go out and find a way to enjoy the things that give you pleasure. It may be that caffeine isn't your friend, but you love it! So once a month give yourself a treat, and set loving intentions for wellbeing. Life is to be enjoyed, and withholding and abstinence are choices. If it brings you pleasure and satisfaction, then do it, without guilt.

If you do have addictions, know that when you focus on the problem, the solution does not arrive. Focus on what it is you want to achieve and the solution will reveal itself. This could be drugs, alcohol, people, sugar or sex – all these things make us feel better in some way, so the trick is to learn what it takes to feel these emotions without the need of the drugs of our choice. Remember balance is the key.

If you believe that addictions can stem from the emotional body and then become a physical symptom, please don't condemn people for needing to medicate in order to function and enjoy life. Some people have to have this in their life in order to learn how to love; having difficulty finding love, they experience a deep desires to escape their painful perceptions. Remember, the further we get away from the miracle of who we are, the more we may need to compensate for this. We may require continued support or repairs. Some people have a stronger constitution and mental capacity, so they can reap havoc, then repair easily, while others are more temperamental and sensitive and they may need extra attention and care. Either way we must pay attention and know what the path is going to be for us. A fine machine runs amazingly well when you put in good fuel, but if the fuel runs out it doesn't matter how fine the machine is, it just won't run. So choose your fuel wisely!

Never say never. You have the right to change your mind.

If you say, "I'll never eat another piece of chocolate again", and one day, maybe even years later, a piece of chocolate comes your way, will you feel guilty it you eat it? Or will you show up new in the moment with a refreshed view? Never implies guilt if you later go back on your word. And then comes anger. Or you didn't eat it, because you wanted to be strong, you wanted to be your word, but the idea of eating it still niggles away at you.

Does 'never' come from the ego, or is it a way to create standards for yourself? I suggest being open, and see what happens. Not reneging on your word to save face may cost you what it is you have always desired, if you deny yourself the pleasure of receiving this next thing because you said never. Think on that!

Never again, I'll never do that...and then you find yourself doing just the thing you said you'd never do! The Law of Attraction will always bring the opportunity to you, especially when there are strong feelings in the mix. When I was younger, I went to the beach with a man who had fuzzy and hairy hands. I said to myself I'd never date a man with hairy hands. Well, the next man I met and fell in love with had hairy hands and I chuckled at the irony of life. I am open to experiencing the things that I resist or that make me uncomfortable because I judge them or can't find the beauty in them. It happens all the time – the thing I say I want the least will be the thing that presents itself the most. So enjoy your 'nevers' as they will also present themselves as openings to the future, and will help you strip away the limitations you set on yourself.

Put your head on straight and look into your physiology.

Since writing this book I have discovered something that has made implementing all these practices even simpler. That's getting my head on straight, literally – it's called upper cervical care where a doctor takes x-rays and checks the upper cervicals that attach your spine and skull. I've worked with Dr. Drew Hall (Blair technique for upper cervical care) for the past 4 years and it has complemented my life so much. If those upper cervicals 1 and 2, known as the atlas and axis, are out of alignment, you may experience chronic symptoms due to adaptation of the subluxation of those vertebrae. Now most of us are off kilter or out of alignment and what I've found since discovering this amazing technique is that I can better manage my emotions. Now everything is cumulative so it all counts. As I've refined my system I've become attuned to the fact that I am less reactive in a tumultuous interaction when my head is properly aligned on my body. Now that's not to say I can bypass all the tools we have spoken of however the clearer you are the easier it is to align to your purpose. Keeping your head on straight opens up the centers for more energy and communication in the central nervous system and when the body is aligned your natural ability to repair will improve exponentially. Another awareness I have seen over the years is keeping the body in homeostasis hormonally, which has a powerful effect on a person's system. If in doubt check it out. There are many methods and modalities that keep the body and system in optimal functioning form. You can do your own research to discover what you'd like to improve upon. Now I believe we can imagine out and visualize a balanced homeostasis and if you are focused you can do anything. However there are times in life where we need outside assistance to rehabilitate the wear and tear from living, so supplements, exercising daily and a spiritual practice of noticing is essential to that balance.

What you put in your body is equally as important as what you speak or put out. Healthy lifestyle and food choices can improve on the alkalinity of your body.

- ☐ Consult a chiropractor
  My personal chiropractors: Dr. Sai-Ling Michael, DC of
  http://healthquesthq.com, and Dr. Drew Hall of
  http://drdrewhall.com for upper cervical care.

- ☐ Practice yoga or martial arts
- ☐ Exercise in general
- ☐ Get live blood analysis (try Dr. Robert Young - Phmiracleliving.com) to see the internal workings of how the body and mind are operating together
- ☐ Work with a life coach / healer / acupuncturist
- ☐ Take sea salt baths
- ☐ Use essential oils
- ☐ Use products that support neurological coherency to counter the effects of the EMFs (lifebeatproducts.com)
- ☐ Take herbs and supplements – my top 4 recommended are E.ssential F.atty A.cids, pro-biotics if you are consuming animal flesh, digestive enzymes, and chlorophyll
- ☐ Attend group seminars on personal development (Tony Robbins, Matrix Energetics)
- ☐ Read books that enhance your spiritual practice (my favorite of all time is Florence Scovel Shinn, "The Game of Life")
- ☐ Consult someone who practices classical homeopathy and find out what your constitutional remedy is
- ☐ Drink alkaline water.

All of these modalities are complementary and can provide a foundation of sustenance that will enhance what your body is already doing.

CHAPTER FOURTEEN SUMMARY:
EXPERIENCE LIFE

1. Make a point of asking for assistance from your guides, angels and the Creator; send the light ahead, using affirmations to make you feel inspired and encouraged.

2. If time is limited, ask: "What can I do right now to improve how I feel?" Find out what is keeping you separate from your joy and from your Creator.

3. Trust and receive, follow your inner promptings, because believing is achieving. For-giving will set you free to receive the next wonderful thing that is showing up in your honor, to greet you in the new place you've arrived. Continue moving forward, and you will continue to grow.

4. Needing it all to becoming it all. It doesn't matter if you have extreme ways of expressing who you are; everyone needs structure within their own system to push them into growth. It's up to you how much and for how long; continue to be loving towards yourself as you do it. The more I love the more I want to be good to my body. Everyone's perception of what is good for them will be different from person to person and from culture to culture.

5. Life is to be enjoyed, so withholding and abstinence are choices. If it brings you pleasure and satisfaction, then do it, without guilt.

6. A fine machine runs amazingly well when you put in good fuel, but if the fuel runs out it doesn't matter how fine the machine is, it just won't run. So choose your fuel wisely!

7. Never say never. You have the right to change your mind!

8. I am open to experiencing the things that I resist or that make me uncomfortable because I judge them or can't find the beauty in them. It happens all the time – the thing I say I want the least will be the thing that presents itself the most.

9. Put your head on straight and look into your physiology. Upper cervical care atlas balancing.

What you put in your body is equally as important as what you speak or put out. Healthy lifestyle and food choices can improve on the alkalinity of your body.

POSTSCRIPT

I truly hope you enjoyed reading *Silver to Gold – The Alchemy of the Feminine Heart*.

A review of this book would be greatly appreciated! Please post a review to your favorite bookseller's website or send it to reviews@TiffanySilverLove.com. Thank you!

Tiffany Silver

http://TiffanySilverLove.com

www.ingramcontent.com/pod-product-compliance
Lightning Source LLC
Chambersburg PA
CBHW060255100426
42742CB00011B/1758